The Best
CHRISTMAS
CRAFTS
Ever!

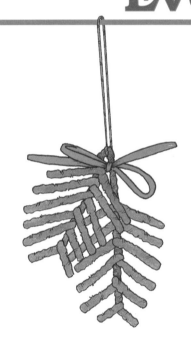

The Best CHRISTMAS CRAFTS Ever!

By Kathy Ross

Illustrated by Sharon Lane Holm

The Millbrook Press Brookfield, Connecticut

Merry Christmas, Julianna!

Library of Congress Cataloging-in-Publication Data

Ross, Kathy (Katharine Reynolds), 1948-
The best Christmas crafts ever! / by Kathy Ross ; illustrated by Sharon
Lane Holm.
p. cm
Summary: Presents more than eighty craft projects with Christmas themes
that can be used as decorations or gifts.

ISBN 0-7613-1688-4

1. Christmas decorations—Juvenile literature. 2. Handicraft—Juvenile literature. [1. Christmas decorations. 2. Handicraft.] I. Holm, Sharon Lane, ill.
II. Title.

TT900.C4 R67494 2002   745.594'12—dc21   2001057950

Published by The Millbrook Press, Inc.
2 Old New Milford Road
Brookfield, Connecticut 06804
www.millbrookpress.com

Printed in Hong Kong

5 4 3 2 1

Contents

Deck the Halls! • 142

Introduction

Dear Readers,

I have always liked to add a little bit of "me" to my Christmas décor in the form of handmade tree ornaments, decorations, and gifts. Over the years, I've built up a wonderful portfolio of delightfully different Christmas craft projects. This is a collection of the best of them.

You'll find dozens of easy-to-make ornaments for your tree, as well as holiday decorating ideas that run the gamut from wonderful to whimsical. And don't forget the homemade gifts! I've included ideas designed to please everyone on your list—there's even something for your pets!

Using only the most basic craft materials and throw-away articles from around the house you can add some real sparkle to your holidays. So, instead of getting out your wallet this season, just get out some scissors and the glue. You'll make Christmas very special for your family and everyone on your gift list. What could be nicer than a little bit of "you"?

Kathy Ross

Make Your Own Gifts

Countdown to Christmas Tree

Make this Christmas tree to give as an early gift.

What you need:

lid from metal cookie tin

white glue

25 sequins of different shapes

green and red construction paper

hole punch

red ribbon or yarn

scissors

pretty trim about as wide as the rim of the lid

pen or pencil

red felt scrap

masking tape

strip of sticky-back magnet

What you do:

1 From the green construction paper, cut a Christmas-tree shape that will fit inside the lid of the metal cookie tin. Put a strip of masking tape down the center of the inside of the lid to create a better gluing surface. Glue the tree into the lid, attaching it to the masking-tape strip.

2 Cut a holder for the base of the tree from the red felt. Glue the holder to the base of the tree. Decorate the holder with trim.

3 Tear a long strip of masking tape in half lengthwise. Cover the inside rim of the lid with the strips. They will help the glue hold.

4 Cut a 12-inch (30-cm) length of red construction paper, making it narrow enough to fit inside the rim of the metal lid. Write the numbers from 1 to 25 across the strip. Glue the strip to the rim below the tree. Glue trim around the rest of the inner rim.

5 Cut a 10-inch (25-cm) length of thin red ribbon or yarn. Put a piece of masking tape on the back of the lid behind the top of the tree. Glue the two ends of the red ribbon or yarn to the masking-tape strip and cover it with more masking-tape strips to secure it.

6 Use the hole punch to punch twenty-five holes from the magnet strip. Peel the paper off each dot and stick it to a sequin. The magnet dot will allow each sequin to stick to the tin lid. Place a sequin over each number on the paper strip.

To use the countdown tree, hang it up, and, starting on December 1, trim the tree with one sequin ornament each day. When all the ornaments are on the tree it will be December 25. Merry Christmas!

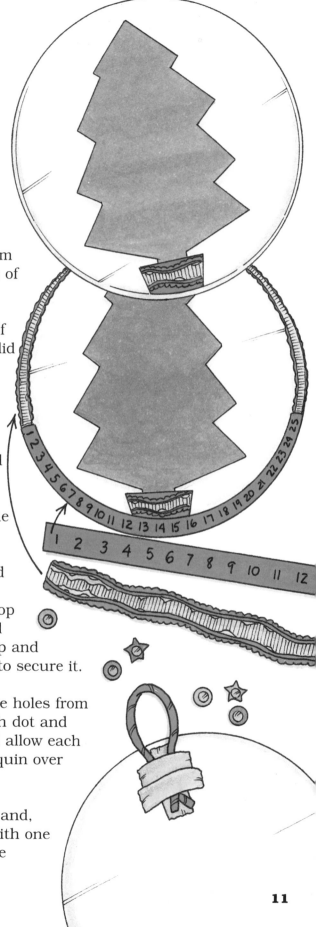

11

Jingle Bell Bracelet

*Put someone special you know in the
Christmas spirit with this holiday bracelet.*

What you need:

bright color sock with
a stretchy cuff

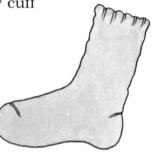

green sparkle stem

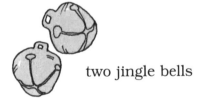

two jingle bells

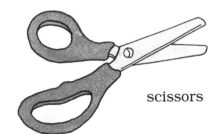

two red beads

scissors

What you do:

1 To make the bracelet, cut a 1-inch (2.5-cm)-wide band from the top of the cuff of the sock.

2 Cut four 2-inch (5-cm) pieces of green sparkle stem.

3 Thread one end of a sparkle stem piece down through the weave of the sock and up again to fasten it to the sock. Thread a jingle bell onto the sparkle stem, then twist the two ends together to secure the bell to the sock bracelet. Do the same thing on the other side of the bracelet.

4 Between the bells on each side of the bracelet thread another piece of sparkle stem. Slide a red bead on each of these and twist the ends together to hold each bead in place.

5 You might want to trim the ends of the sparkle stems so that they are all about the same length.

Try making more than one of these bracelets in different colors. You might also have other ideas for what decorations you attach. These bracelets can be worn on ankles as well as wrists. Whoever you give them to will look and sound very Christmasy!

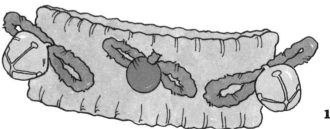

13

Marker Cap Lapel Pin

Here is just the gift to make for your favorite aunt!

What you need:

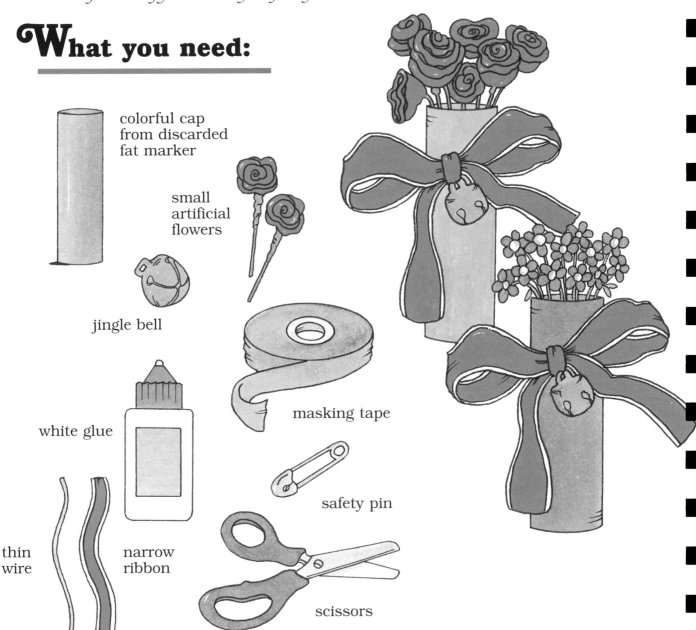

colorful cap from discarded fat marker

small artificial flowers

jingle bell

white glue

masking tape

safety pin

thin wire

narrow ribbon

scissors

14

What you do:

1 Turn the marker cap so that the opening is on the top to form a little container for the flowers. Put a small piece of masking tape just above the middle of one side of the marker cap.

2 Glue the back of the closed safety pin to the tape and secure it over the glue with another piece of masking tape. This will be the back of the lapel pin.

3 Cut an 8-inch (20-cm) length of ribbon. Thread one end of the ribbon through the closed safety pin on the back of the marker cap. Tie the ribbon in a pretty bow. Trim the ends as needed.

4 To attach the jingle bell to the bow, thread a piece of wire through the top of the jingle bell and under the bow. Tie the two ends of the wire together to secure the bell. Trim off the ends of the wire.

5 If necessary, trim the stems of the flowers to make them fit nicely in the marker cap container. Squeeze some glue into the container. Arrange the flowers in the container by adjusting the ends in the glue.

When the glue has dried you will have a lovely lapel pin. You might want to make more than one of this simple but attractive holiday gift.

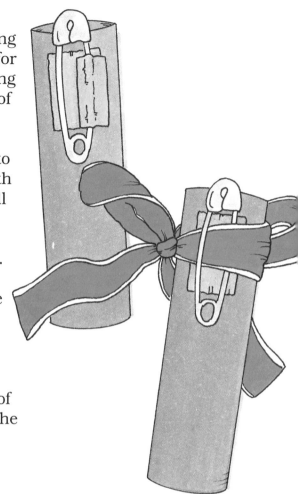

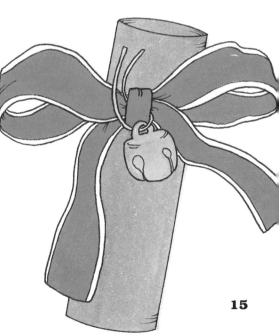

Snowman Antenna Ball

This is the perfect gift for anyone who has trouble finding his or her car in a crowded mall parking lot.

What you need:

2-inch (5-cm) Styrofoam ball

child's sock

pencil

colored map pins

big sequin or button

straight pins

scissors

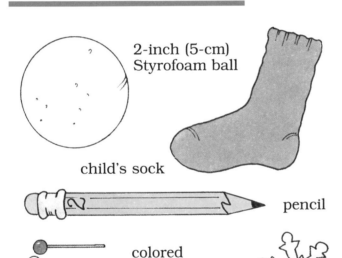

tiny red pom-pom

white glue

³⁄₄-inch (2-cm) red pom-pom

What you do:

1 Cut the foot off the sock, leaving the heel end with the cuff. This will be a hat for the Styrofoam ball head.

2 Roll the cut end of the foot up at least twice to make a band on the hat. Roll the end until the hat is about 2½ inches (6 cm) long.

3 Put the hat on the Styrofoam ball and secure it with straight pins. Because the car antenna will need to go through the center of the ball to attach it, put all the pins in at an angle so they do not cross the center of the ball and block the way of the antenna.

4 Glue the larger red pom-pom to the end of the hat. Use a map pin to attach a pretty sequin or button to the band of the hat to decorate it.

5 Stick two map pins in the Styrofoam ball below the brim of the hat for eyes. Attach the tiny red pom-pom with a straight pin for the nose.

6 Use the point of the pencil to poke a small hole through the bottom of the head to show where the antenna should go.

A snowman antenna ball is not only a practical gift but a fun one as well.

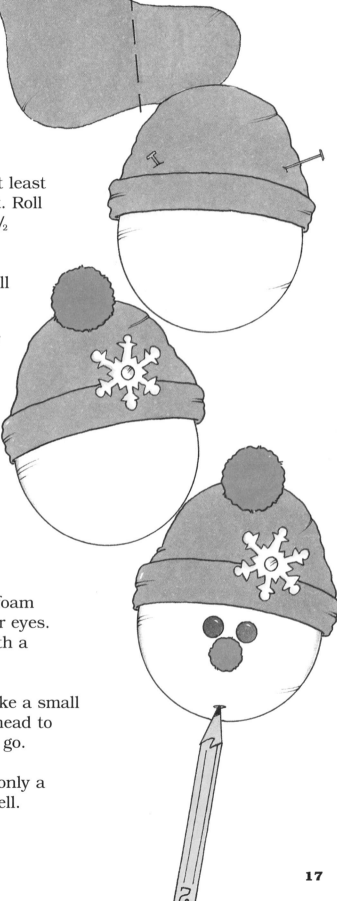

Padded Envelope Trivet

A festive trivet would be a welcome gift for anyone's holiday table.

What you need:

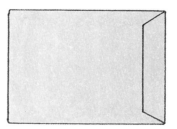

8½ - by 11-inch
(22- by 28-cm)
padded envelope

blue glue
gel

two 9- by 12-inch
(23- by 30-cm) felt pieces
of the same color

rickrack trim

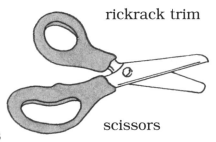

scissors

stapler

felt scraps in
other colors

What you do:

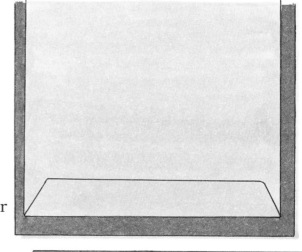

1 If the envelope has been used, pull out any staples and trim the open end so that it is straight across if necessary.

2 Set the padded envelope in the center of one of the felt pieces so that the edge of the felt shows all around the outside of the envelope. Set the second felt piece over the envelope and exactly matching the edges of the bottom felt piece. Staple the two felt pieces together all around the edges with the envelope in between them. The best way to do this is to put one staple in the center of each end, then one in the center of each side to hold the envelope in place between the felt pieces. Then go back and staple the open areas around the trivet.

3 Decorate the trivet by gluing rickrack all around the edges over the staples.

4 Cut one or more pretty holiday shapes from the felt scraps to glue in one corner of the trivet.

You can make a whole set of trivets using a different-size padded envelope for each one.

Priority Mail Box Video Holder

A small priority mail carton is just the right size for storing a special Christmas video.

What you need:

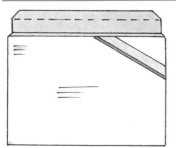

6- by 9- by 2-inch
(15- by 23- by 5-cm)-
size priority mail box

fabric

white
glue

two paper
fasteners

bias tape that goes
with the fabric

thin ribbon

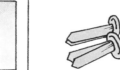

paintbrush

scissors

Styrofoam tray or egg
carton for drying

masking
tape

newspaper
to work on

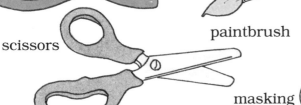

What you do:

1 You will need an unused priority mail box. These boxes are free at the post office and come flat. Leave the box flat until after you have covered it with fabric. Do not remove the white strip on the flap of the box. Cut a piece of fabric big enough to cover the outside of the box. It does not have to fit exactly. You can trim the edges after the glue dries. Cut a slit in the fabric on each side where there is a slit in the box to slip the tabs in to assemble.

2 Cover the outer surface of the box with strips of masking tape to create a better gluing surface. You do not have to cover the entire surface. A few crisscrossed pieces of tape over each section of the box will be fine.

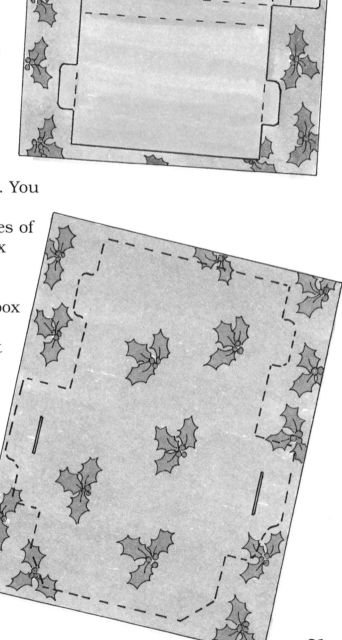

3 Cover the entire outside of the box with glue, using the paintbrush to spread it evenly. Carefully set the fabric on the box over the glue, making sure it is as smooth as possible and the slits in the fabric are lined up with the slits in the box. Put the box on the Styrofoam tray or egg carton to dry. This will keep it from sticking to the newspaper.

4 When the project is dry, trim off the extra fabric.

5 Assemble the box and secure the sides and tabs with glue.

6 Finish the edges of the box by gluing on bias tape.

7 Poke a hole in the center of the flap. Hold the flap closed and poke another hole about 1 inch (2.5 cm) below the center of the closed flap. Put a paper fastener in each hole and secure it by bending the two arms in opposite directions.

8 Cut a 10-inch (25-cm) length of ribbon. Tie the ribbon around the paper fastener on the flap of the box. Close the flap and tie the ribbon in a knot, then a bow, around the second paper fastener. The ribbon should be able to slip on and off the second fastener to open and close the box.

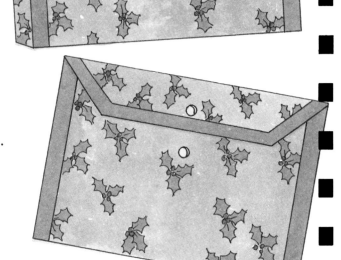

This is a great gift for the video taker in your family. This year's Christmas video can be stored in the video holder, ready to be enjoyed next Christmas.

Decorated Tape Dispenser

Just about anyone would find this decorated tape dispenser an attractive and useful holiday gift.

What you need:

new roll of cellophane tape in a clear plastic dispenser

white glue

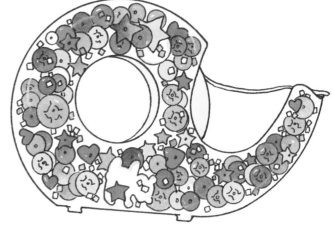

Styrofoam tray to work on

small mixed sequins

What you do:

1 Remove the roll of tape from the dispenser and set aside. Take out the paper insert and discard.

2 Cover the back inside of the plastic tape dispenser with white glue. Cover the glue with assorted sequins.

3 Leave the dispenser laying flat on the Styrofoam tray until the glue dries completely. This could take as long as a week.

4 When the glue is dry, put the tape back in the dispenser.

Can you think of other ways to decorate the inside of the tape dispenser? Maybe some holiday wrapping paper or colored glue?

23

Stuffed Snowman Friend

Here is a project sure to delight your younger brother or sister.

What you need:

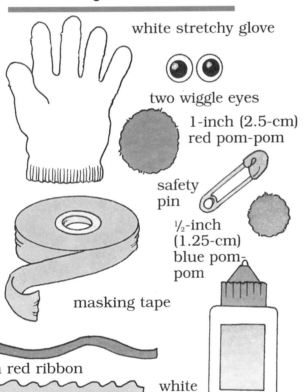

white stretchy glove

two wiggle eyes

1-inch (2.5-cm) red pom-pom

safety pin

½-inch (1.25-cm) blue pom-pom

masking tape

thin red ribbon

thin trim or rickrack

white glue

scissors

fiberfill

thin string or yarn

two candy canes

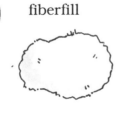

24

What you do:

1 Turn the middle finger of the glove inside out up inside the glove. The two fingers on each side of the missing finger will become legs of the snowman, the thumb and little finger will become arms, and the hand portion will form the body and head. Stuff the entire snowman with fiberfill.

2 Cut a 10-inch (25-cm) length of ribbon. Tie it around the hand portion of the glove just above the thumb to form the neck of the snowman. Tie the ribbon in a pretty bow and trim the ends.

3 Cut a 6-inch (15-cm) piece of thin string or yarn. Tie the top of the glove closed about 1 inch (2.5 cm) below the cuff. Trim off the ends of the yarn. Fold the cuff down to form a hat for the snowman.

4 Glue trim around the brim of the hat. Glue the red pom-pom to the top of the hat. Put small squares of masking tape on the head of the snowman where you want to glue the eyes and the nose. Put a square of masking tape on the back of each wiggle eye and glue them in place. Put a piece of masking tape on one side of the blue pom-pom and glue the tape side to the snowman to make the nose.

5 Tie two candy canes together with a piece of the thin red ribbon. Use the safety pin to pin the snowman's hands together. Slip the candy canes behind the pinned hands to look like the snowman is holding them.

Slip a piece of yarn through the ribbon at the back of the snowman and tie the two ends together to make a hanger if you would like this snowman to hang on the tree.

25

Decorated Wrapped Coins

Here is a fun way to give the gift of money.

What you need:

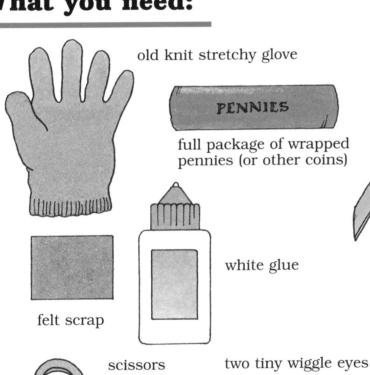

old knit stretchy glove

PENNIES

full package of wrapped pennies (or other coins)

white glue

felt scrap

scissors

two tiny wiggle eyes

two tiny pom-poms

½-inch (1.25-cm) wide ribbon

What you do:

1 Cut a piece a little more than 1 inch (2.5 cm) long off the tip of the thumb of the glove. Roll the cut end of the tip up to form the brim of a little hat. Glue the hat to one end of the wrapped coins. Glue one of the tiny pom-poms to the top of the hat.

2 Glue the two wiggle eyes on the side of the wrapper just below the hat brim. Glue the second pom-pom on below the eyes for a nose.

3 Cut the longest finger off the glove. Cut the tip off the finger so you have a knit tube. Slip the tube over the wrapped coins to make clothes.

4 Fold the felt scrap in half and cut an oval shape at an angle 1½ inches (4 cm) long with one end on the fold. Open the oval up and glue it to the bottom of the wrapper with the two oval halves sticking out from the front to look like feet.

5 Cut a 6-inch (15-cm) length of ribbon. Tie the ribbon around the wrapper just below the nose to look like a scarf.

If you have any siblings or baby-sitters in college, a roll of quarters for the washing machines makes a great gift.

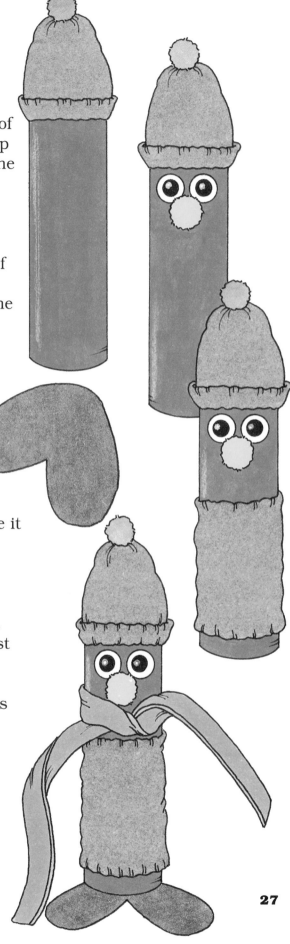

Holiday Stamp Holder

This idea for a holiday stamp holder can be used to make stamp dispensers for any time of the year.

What you need:

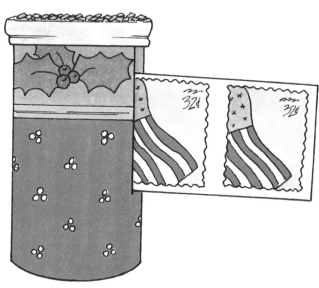

plastic film
canister with lid

scissors

masking tape

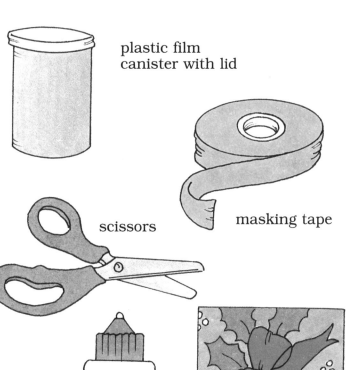

white
glue

pretty wrapping
paper

tiny sequins
and glitter

What you do:

1 Cover the outer surface of the film canister with masking tape to create a better gluing surface. Cover the top of the lid with tape also.

2 Cut a slit about three quarters of the way down the side of the canister.

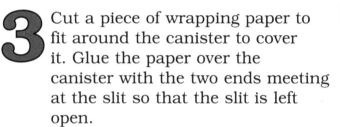

3 Cut a piece of wrapping paper to fit around the canister to cover it. Glue the paper over the canister with the two ends meeting at the slit so that the slit is left open.

4 Cover the top of the lid with glue. Sprinkle the glue with the sequins. Dust with glitter to help fill in any gaps.

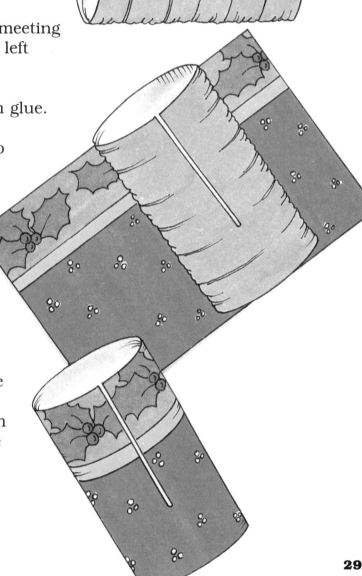

To use the dispenser, just slip a roll of stamps in the canister with the end of the roll sticking out of the slit in the side. Snap the top on the canister. As stamps are needed, the roll can be pulled out from the side of the canister.

Sticker Star Tree Pin

This tiny tree looks great worn on a coat.

What you need:

gold sticker stars

piece of gold sparkle stem

pin back or safety pin

white glue

plastic wrap

scissors

masking tape

What you do:

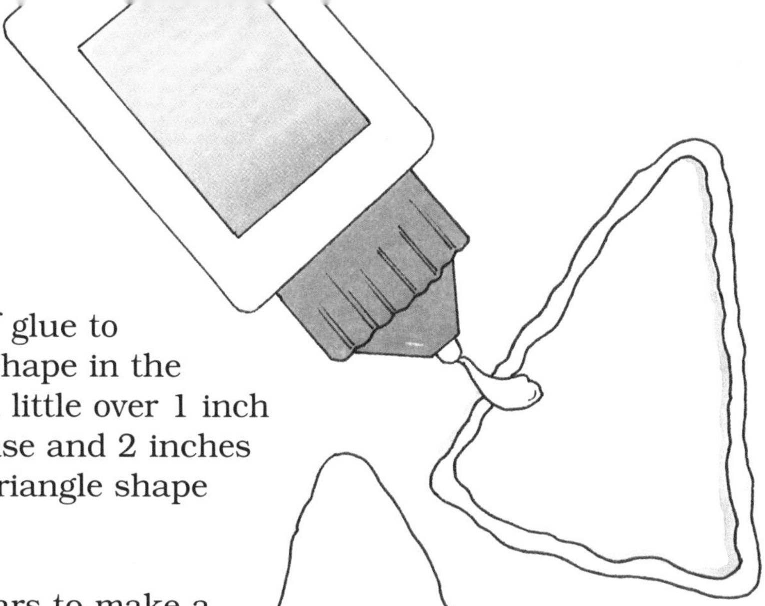

1 Use a squeeze bottle of glue to draw a small triangle shape in the plastic wrap. Make it a little over 1 inch (2.5 cm) wide at the base and 2 inches (5 cm) tall. Fill in the triangle shape with glue.

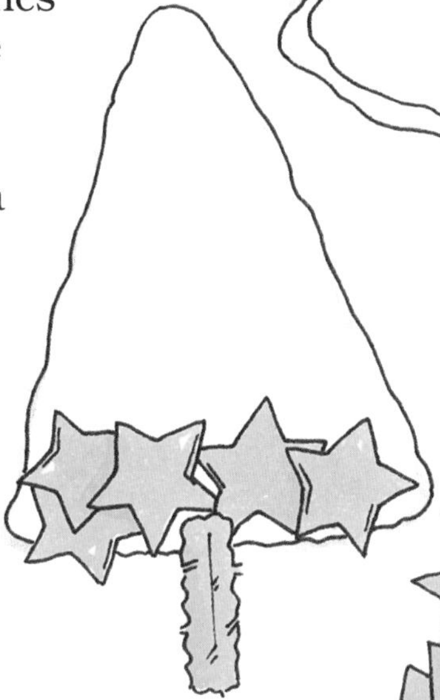

2 Use the gold sticker stars to make a tree, starting at the bottom and working up to the point.

3 Cut a ½-inch (1.25-cm) piece of the sparkle stem. Stick one end of the piece in the glue at the center of the bottom of the tree to form the base. Let the glue dry completely on a flat surface, undisturbed.

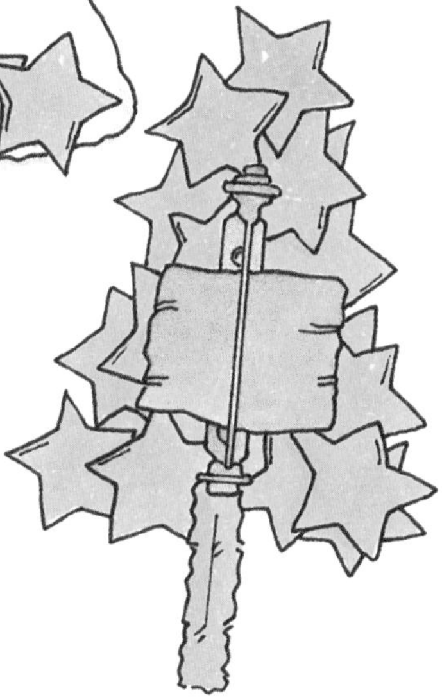

4 When the glue has dried, peel the tree off the plastic wrap. Use the scissors to trim off any excess glue that has run off the sides around the stars.

5 Put a small piece of masking tape on the back of the tree to create a better gluing surface. Glue on a safety pin or pin back. Put another piece of masking tape over the back of the safety pin or pin back to hold it in place while the glue dries.

You might want to make your tree with green stars or all different colors. How pretty!

31

Jingle Bell Hair Snaps

These hair snaps look and sound like Christmas!

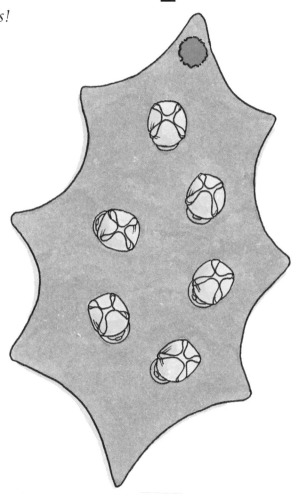

What you need:

6 snaps
(size no. 1/0
work well)

spool
of fine
wire

six jingle bells

white glue

scissors

small red
pom-pom

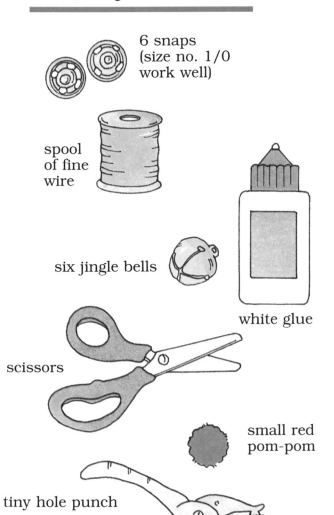

tiny hole punch

green construction paper

32

What you do:

1 Cut a 6-inch (15-cm) piece of wire. Unsnap a snap. Tie one end of the wire through the top part of the snap.

2 Thread a jingle bell onto the wire. Thread the wire down through another hole in the snap. Weave the wire in and out of the holes in the snap a few times to secure the bell. Tie off the end of the wire and trim off any extra. Use the top half of six snaps to make six jingle bell snaps.

3 For gift giving, make something pretty to attach the bells to. One idea is to cut a 4-inch (10-cm) holly leaf from the green construction paper.

4 Glue the red pom-pom to one point to look like a holly berry.

5 Punch a hole in the leaf for each hair snap you made. Attach the hair snaps to the holly by joining the top and bottom of each snap together through a hole in the leaf.

Each jingle bell hair snap can easily be snapped onto a lock of hair for a charming and musical holiday hair decoration.

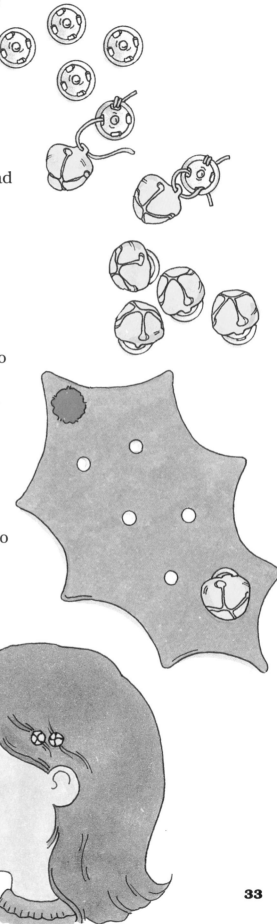

Beaded Spoon

Brighten up someone's holiday table
with this attractive project.

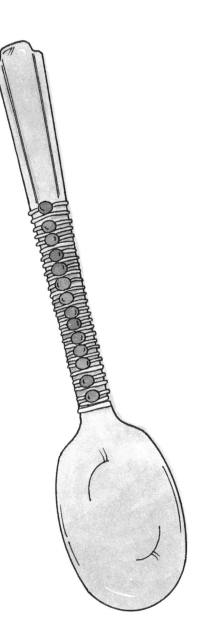

What you need:

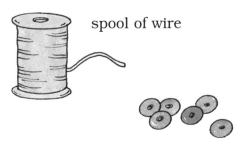

spool of wire

large-size seed beads in
your choice of colors

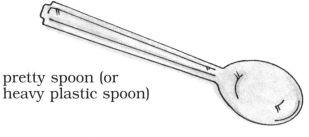

pretty spoon (or
heavy plastic spoon)

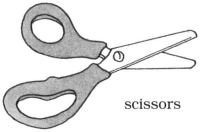

scissors

What you do:

1 Cut off a 16-inch (41-cm) piece of wire. How much you actually need will depend on the size of your spoon and how much of the handle you decide to decorate.

2 Wrap one end of the wire around the top of the spoon handle, just below the bowl, to secure the wire to the top of the spoon.

3 Thread a bead onto the wire so that it rests on the front of the handle. Wrap the wire snugly around the handle a couple of times, then add another bead. Continue to do this until about half the handle is decorated. If you go further, the decoration will interfere with the use of the spoon.

4 Trim off any extra wire and tuck the end under the wrapped wire to secure.

The colorful seed beads turn an ordinary spoon into a beautiful gift.

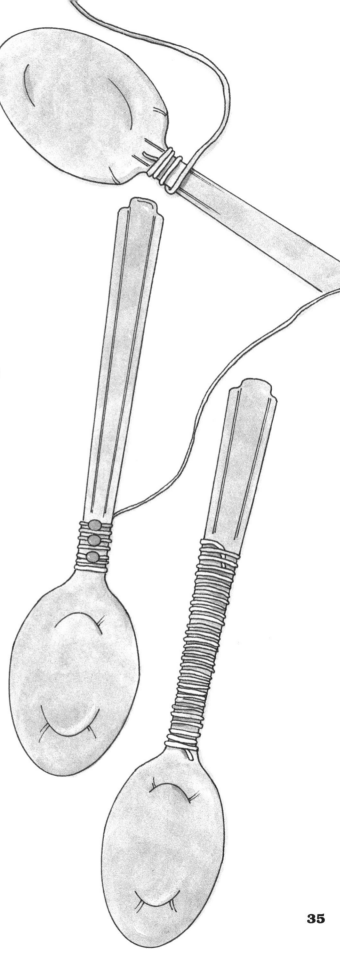

Tissue Box Angel

Turn an ordinary tissue box into a pretty Christmas angel for an extra-special gift.

What you need:

new square box of tissues

white coffee filter

aluminum foil

metallic trim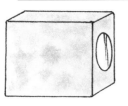

golf tee

big red sequin

white glue

yarn bits for hair

markers

scissors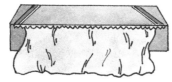

12-inch (30-cm) pipe cleaner in same shade as construction paper

masking tape

two holly leaf sequins

construction paper in skin tone of your choice

36

What you do:

1 Tear off a square of aluminum foil. Fold it in half and cut out a wing shape on the fold about 7 inches (18 cm) tall and 5 inches (13 cm) wide. Open the foil so you have two wings attached at the center. Put a piece of masking tape across the back center of the wings. This helps make a better gluing surface.

2 Turn the tissue box on its side so that the tissue hangs down one side. Put a strip of masking tape above the opening. Glue the wings on the box above the opening.

3 Cut the coffee filter in half. Fold each piece into thirds for the sleeves of the angel. Slide a sleeve on each end of the pipe cleaner, pointed end first, until they meet at the center. Glue the bottom of each sleeve together. Glue the sleeves over the center of the wings.

4 Cut a 2-inch (5-cm) circle from the construction paper. Use the markers to draw on a face. Glue on yarn bits for hair. Glue the holly leaves and red sequin berry in the angel hair. You can also cut the holly decoration from paper. Glue the head in the center of the wings and sleeves.

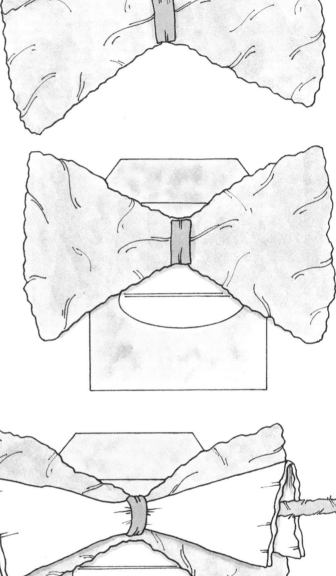

5 Fold the two sleeves toward the center of the angel. Wrap the two ends of the pipe cleaner around the golf tee to look like the angel has a trumpet.

6 Glue metallic trim on each sleeve to decorate them.

This angel tissue box sits on the edge of a shelf with the tissue dress hanging down. When one tissue is removed, another will appear until the box is empty. What a lovely way to decorate a tissue box for the Christmas season!

Zipper Pull

Whoever gets this little treasure will jingle through the rest of the winter.

What you need:

jingle bell

¼-inch (0.6-cm) beads

sparkle stem

paper clip

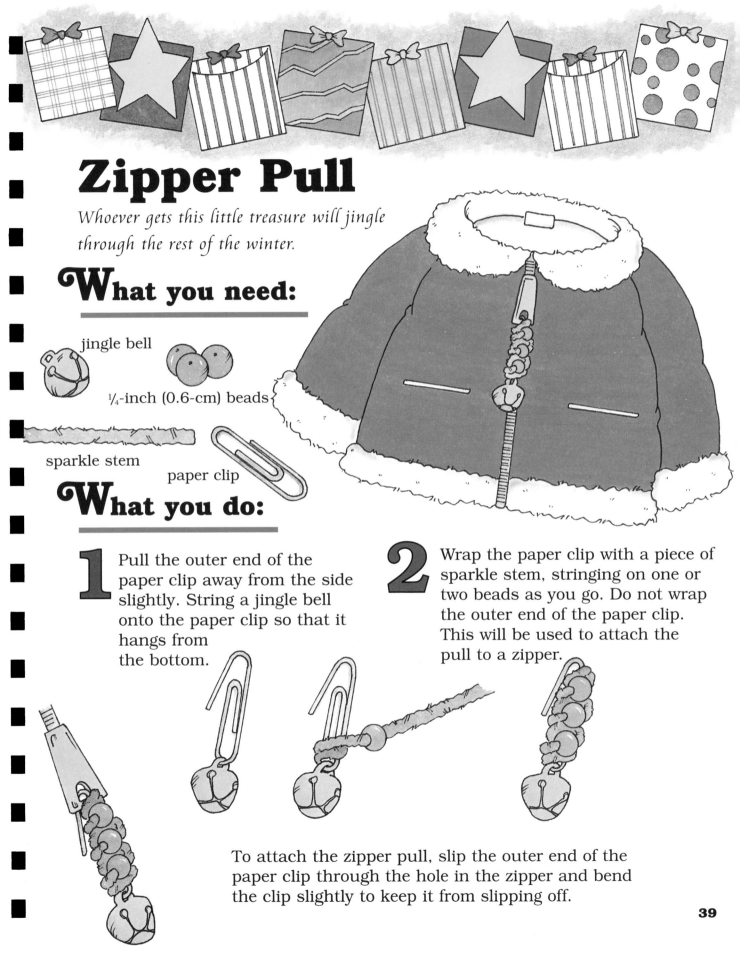

What you do:

1 Pull the outer end of the paper clip away from the side slightly. String a jingle bell onto the paper clip so that it hangs from the bottom.

2 Wrap the paper clip with a piece of sparkle stem, stringing on one or two beads as you go. Do not wrap the outer end of the paper clip. This will be used to attach the pull to a zipper.

To attach the zipper pull, slip the outer end of the paper clip through the hole in the zipper and bend the clip slightly to keep it from slipping off.

Paw Pads

Have you made a Christmas present for your favorite dog friend yet?

roll of white
paper towels

jingle bell

thin red ribbon

scissors

stapler

black marker

What you do:

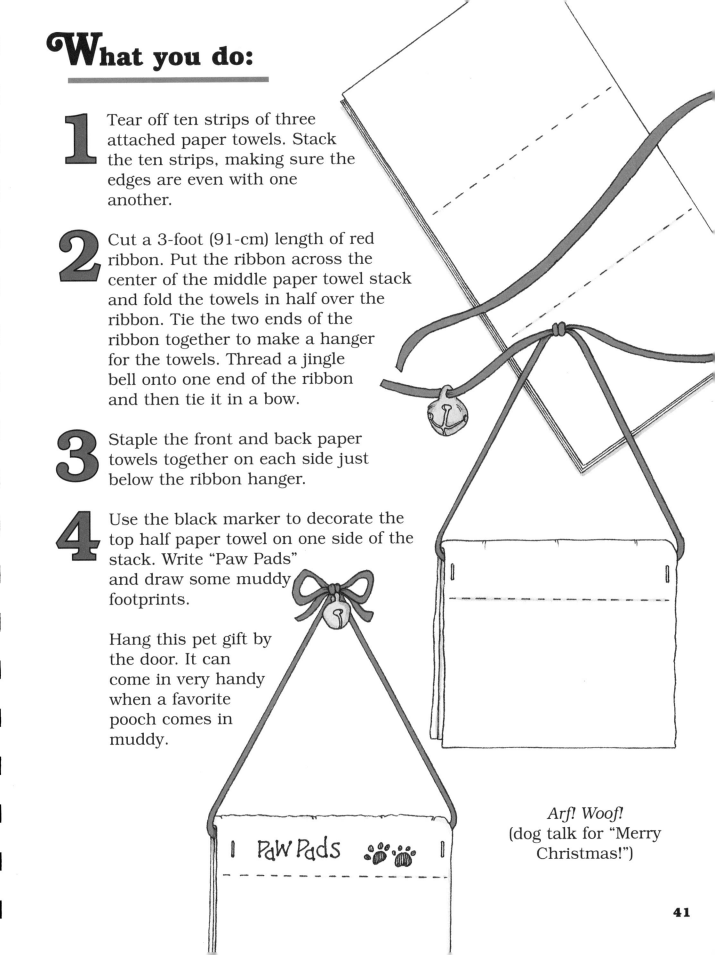

1 Tear off ten strips of three attached paper towels. Stack the ten strips, making sure the edges are even with one another.

2 Cut a 3-foot (91-cm) length of red ribbon. Put the ribbon across the center of the middle paper towel stack and fold the towels in half over the ribbon. Tie the two ends of the ribbon together to make a hanger for the towels. Thread a jingle bell onto one end of the ribbon and then tie it in a bow.

3 Staple the front and back paper towels together on each side just below the ribbon hanger.

4 Use the black marker to decorate the top half paper towel on one side of the stack. Write "Paw Pads" and draw some muddy footprints.

Hang this pet gift by the door. It can come in very handy when a favorite pooch comes in muddy.

Arf! Woof!
(dog talk for "Merry Christmas!")

PaW Pads

41

Christmas Cat Collar

Kitty cat wants a Christmas present, too!

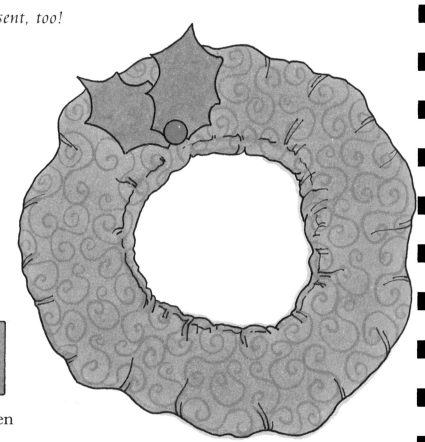

What you need:

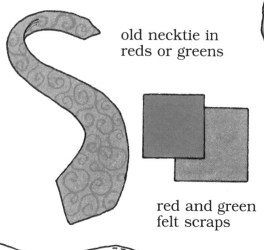

old necktie in
reds or greens

red and green
felt scraps

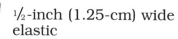

½-inch (1.25-cm) wide
elastic

safety pin

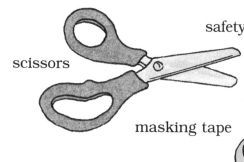

scissors

masking tape

blue glue gel

What you do:

1 Cut a piece of elastic long enough to fit loosely around the cat's neck and overlap 1 inch (2.5 cm). Do not stretch the elastic at all.

2 Cut the narrow half of the necktie off. Cut off the point at the end.

3 Put a safety pin on one end of the elastic. Use the pin as a holder to thread the elastic through the strip of necktie. Gather the necktie strip over the elastic, then pin the two ends of the elastic together, overlapping the ends about 1 inch (2.5 cm). Wrap the safety-pinned ends with masking tape to be sure the pin will not open and poke the kitty cat. (*Meow!*)

4 Fold one of the cut ends of the necktie strip inside itself to create a clean edge. If the seam is coming unraveled secure it with a small amount of glue. Slip the folded end of the strip over the other end and glue it in place. Do not use any more glue then you need to because necktie fabric stains easily.

5 Cut two holly leaves from the green felt. Cut a holly berry from the red felt. Glue the two leaves over the spot where the two ends of the necktie are glued together. Glue the red berry in the center top of the two leaves.

This little gift will have kitty looking her Christmas best! *Meow! Purr!* (You guessed it! Kitty talk for "Merry Christmas!")

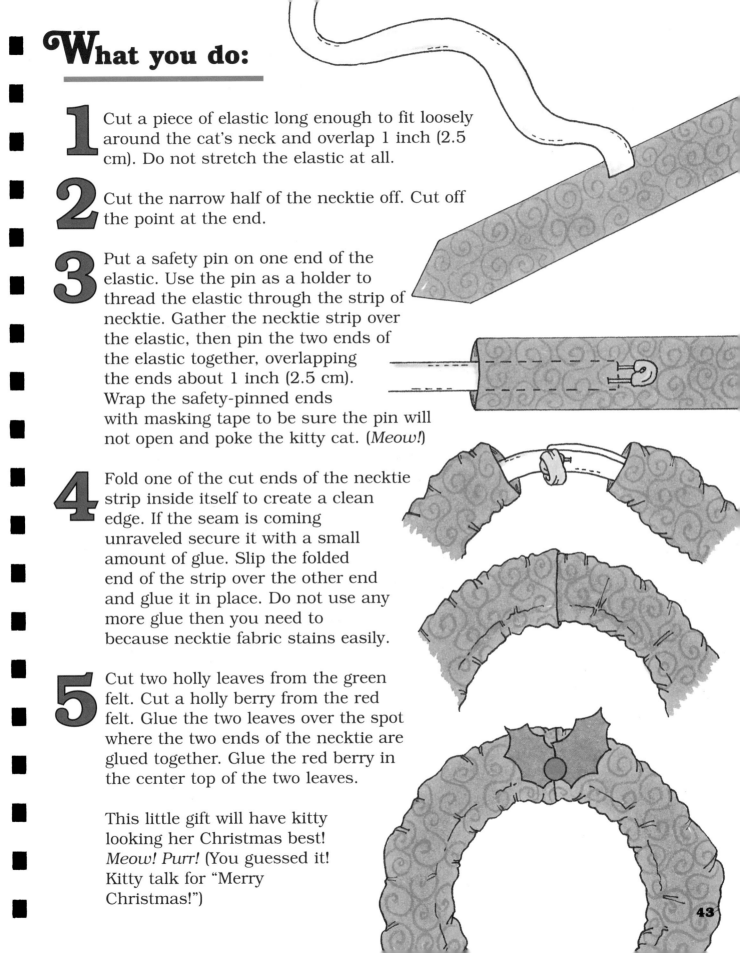

Catalog Christmas Tree

Here is a great way to use some of those Christmas catalogs that come in the mail.

What you need:

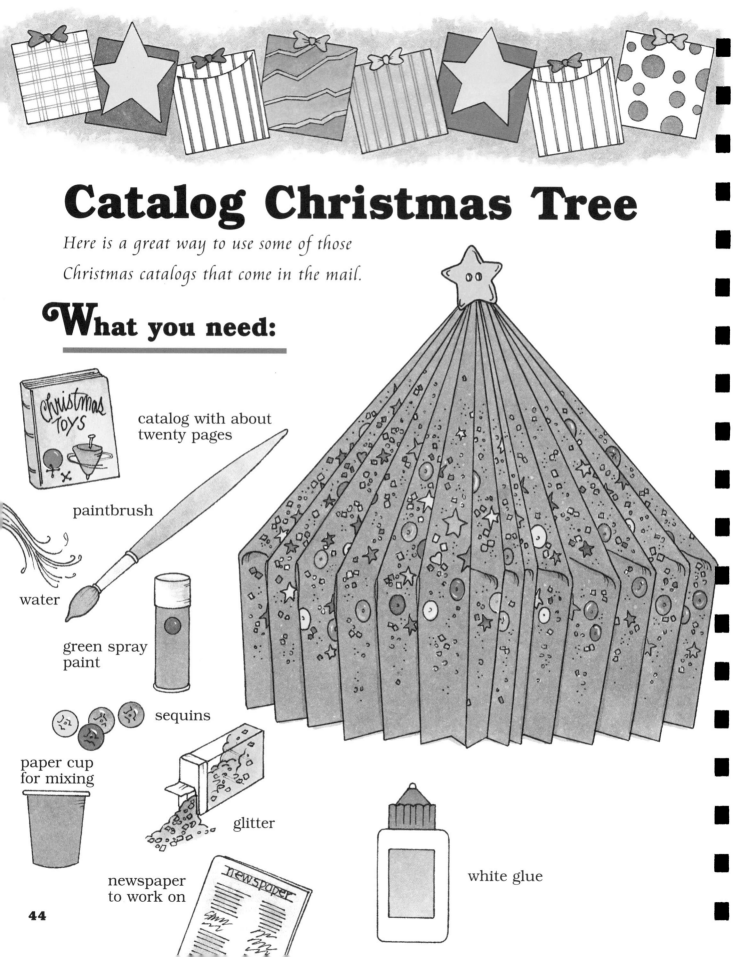

catalog with about twenty pages

paintbrush

water

green spray paint

sequins

paper cup for mixing

glitter

newspaper to work on

white glue

What you do:

1 Fold the top corner of the inside cover of the catalog down in a triangle to the inside center of the catalog. Fold the top corner of the back cover in to the center of the catalog.

2 Fold the top corner of each page of the catalog down to the center of the catalog, making sure you fold each page on the same side. When you are done folding, you will have a nice triangle-shaped tree that will stand by itself.

3 Because so many catalogs have shiny pages, poster paint is not a good choice for this project. It will peel off most catalogs, making quite a mess. It is best to ask an adult to help you spray-paint the tree green. Spray paint must be either done by an adult or with adult supervision.

4 When the paint has dried, you can decorate the tree. Mix two parts glue with one part water in the paper cup. Paint the front of the tree with the watery glue, then sprinkle it with sequins and glitter. If you do not have a large star-shaped sequin for the top, make a star from cut paper. Cover it with glitter to make it shiny, then glue it to the top of your tree.

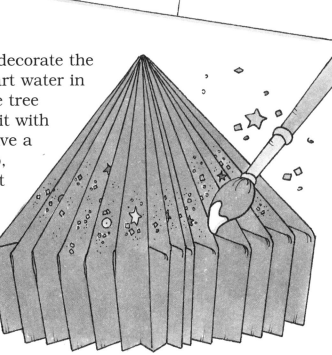

The size of your tree will depend on the size of the catalog it is made from. One or more of these sturdy trees will make a lovely table display that will be enjoyed for many Christmas holidays to come.

45

Baby's First Christmas Ornament

This ornament makes a sweet memento for a new baby.

What you need:

white paper napkin

green paper scrap

red sequin

thin red ribbon

jingle bell

stapler

marker

white glue

hole punch

scissors

46

What you do:

1 Fold a paper napkin square into a triangle. Pull the two ends off the long side of the triangle together, then fold the last corner up over it, just like a folded diaper. Hold the three corners together with a staple.

2 Cut two holly leaves from the green paper. Glue them over the staple at the front of the diaper. Glue a red sequin over the center of the two leaves for a holly berry.

3 Cut a 2-inch (5-cm)-square piece of green paper. Use the marker to write "Baby's First Christmas" and the year on the paper. Punch a hole in the corner of the paper. Also punch a hole on one side of the diaper.

4 Cut a 6-inch (15-cm) length of ribbon. Thread one end through the hole in the diaper, then tie the two ends together to form a hanger. Thread a jingle bell and the paper onto one of the tied ribbon ends, then tie the ends in a knot around the bell and the paper to hold them in place.

You can use a colored or printed napkin for this project, too.

47

Christmas Candy Ball

Just about anyone would be happy
to receive this yummy gift.

What you need:

2½-inch (6-cm)
Styrofoam ball

straight pins

bag of twist-wrapped candy

white glue

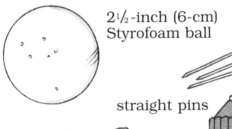

garland

masking tape

ribbon

scissors

plastic laundry
bottle cap

What you do:

1 Turn the cap open-end-up and put masking tape around the open edge to create a better gluing surface. Cover the taped edge with glue. Push the Styrofoam ball into the cap as far as it will go, embedding the glue-covered edge of the cap into the ball.

2 Starting at the bottom of the ball, use a pin to attach the paper at one end of a piece of candy to the ball so that it hangs down over the edge of the lid. Hang candies all the way around the ball, then start a new row above the bottom row. Continue attaching candies until the entire ball is covered.

3 Cut a 2-foot (61-cm) length of garland. Starting at the bottom of the ball, tuck the garland randomly between the candies, going around and around the ball and working toward the top. If you need more garland, just cut another piece. The garland should stay in place between the candies without additional pins, but you can use more pins if you feel they are needed.

4 Tie a ribbon in a bow around the lid just below the candy ball.

5 This can be done with any kind of candy that is wrapped in cellophane that is twisted at both ends.

Yum-yum!

Photo Elf Pin

I'm sure your mom would love it if you made her one of these pins to wear on her coat this Christmas season.

What you need:

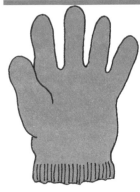
old knit glove or mitten in red, white, or green

white glue

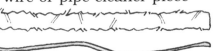
wire or pipe cleaner piece

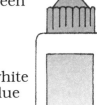
1-inch (2.5-cm)-wide plastic cap

scissors

masking tape

pin backing
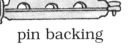

cotton ball

trim

jingle bell

photo with your face about 1 inch (2.5 cm) around

What you do:

1 Glue the cotton ball inside the cap to fill it. Cut the picture of your face from the photo and glue it over the cotton ball.

2 Cut the thumb off the mitten or glove to make the hat. Attach the jingle bell to the tip of the thumb by threading a piece of pipe cleaner or wire through the top of the bell and the knit fabric, then twisting the two ends together. Trim off any extra pipe cleaner or wire from the ends.

3 Roll the cut end of the thumb up to form a brim for the hat. Put glue on the top part of the cap and photo, then slip the hat on over the glued portion.

4 Glue a band of trim around the hat just above the brim.

5 Wrap the back of the pin back with masking tape to create a better gluing surface. Glue the pin back to the back of the cap.

Now your mom can wear her favorite little "elf" right on her coat collar.

Trim the Tree

Christmas Story Frame Ornaments

Make a series of frame ornaments to tell the Christmas story.

What you need:

old Christmas cards

foil cupcake cups

glitter

gold thread

white glue

cereal box cardboard

masking tape

scissors

construction paper

pencil

newspaper to work on

What you do:

1 Cut the bottom out of one cupcake cup. Trace the circle shape on the cereal box and cut it out to use as a pattern.

2 Find pictures on old Christmas cards to tell the Christmas story. Choose scenes that will fit in the circle pattern.

3 Use the pattern to trace around each scene. Cut out the scenes.

4 Put a strip of masking tape inside the bottom of each foil cup you will be using. This will create a better gluing surface.

5 Glue a scene in each cup. Rub glue around the edge of each scene, and sprinkle it with glitter.

6 Use the cardboard pattern to cut a construction paper circle for the back of each ornament.

7 For each ornament, cut a 5-inch (13-cm) piece of gold thread. Glue both ends of the thread to the back of the ornament so that the loop forms a hanger at the top of the scene. Glue a construction paper circle over the back of the ornament.

What a pretty way to tell the story of baby Jesus.

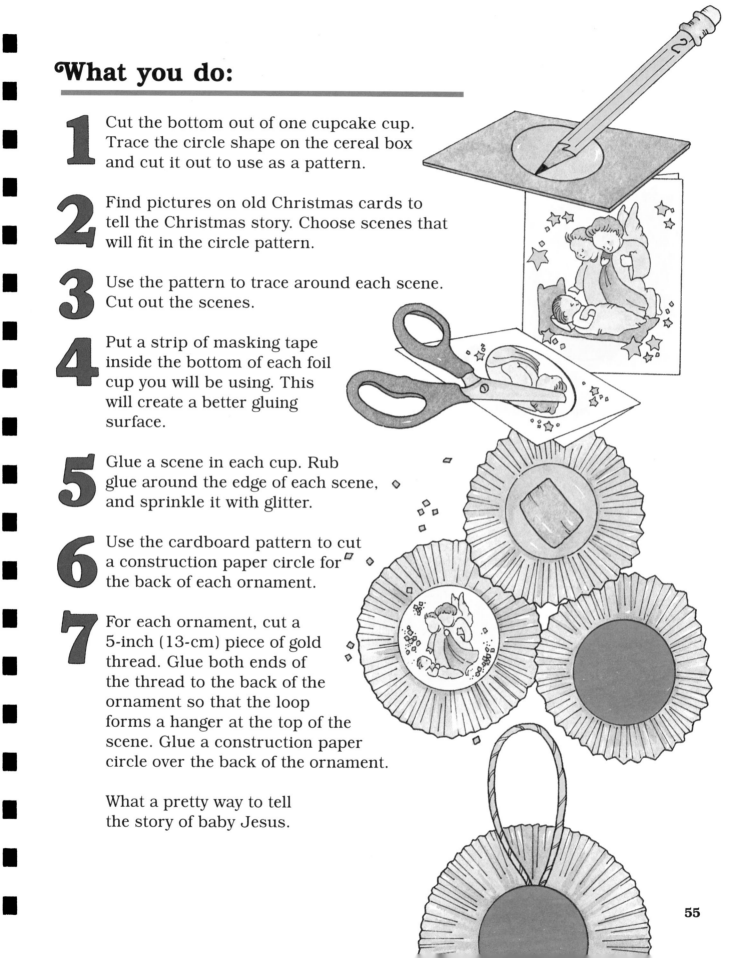

Santa-Down-the-Chimney Ornament

Send Santa down the chimney and back up again with this ornament.

What you need:

small sliding matchbox

red felt

fiberfill

2-inch (5-cm) tall Santa picture or sticker

scissors

blue glue gel

green yarn

masking tape

hole punch

black permanent marker

What you do:

1 Cut a piece of felt large enough to wrap and cover the outer part of the matchbox. Glue the felt in place. Use a black marker to draw bricks on the felt to make it look like a chimney.

2 Glue fiberfill around one open edge to look like snow around the top of the chimney.

3 Punch a hole in the top and bottom end of the inner box.

4 Cut a 12-inch (30-cm) piece of yarn. Fold the yarn in half and knot it together toward the two ends. Thread the yarn up through the two holes in the inner box so that the knotted end hangs out one end and the loop is at the other as a hanger for the ornament. Glue the yarn inside the box, then cover it with masking tape.

5 Glue the Santa picture inside the bottom of the box, with his head toward the loop. If you don't have a picture or sticker, you can draw your own. Put the inner box back inside the outer box.

Just pull on the bottom or top of the yarn to make Santa go up or down the chimney.

Plate Ornament

Holiday plates can be turned into adorable three-dimensional ornaments.

What you need:

package of
paper plates
with a Christ-
mas object or
figure in the
center

scissors

yarn and trims in
Christmas colors

white glue

glitter

small wiggle eyes

small
pom-poms

cotton balls

What you do:

1 Cut the figure out of the center of two identical paper plates.

2 Cut a 4-inch (10-cm) piece of yarn.

3 Cut three ½-inch (1½-cm) squares from the plate scraps and glue them together in a stack.

4 Glue the stack to the center front of one figure and the back of the other to join them together. The double figure will give the ornament a three-dimensional look. At the same time, glue the two ends of the yarn between the top of the two figures to form a hanger.

5 Decorate the front figure by highlighting it with trims, glitter, cotton, pom-poms, and wiggle eyes. What you use will depend on the picture on the plates you use. If you cut out a Christmas tree, you might want to use sequins, and if you cut out a Santa head, you could cover the beard with cotton.

Decorating plate ornaments gives you lots of room to add your own creative finishing touches!

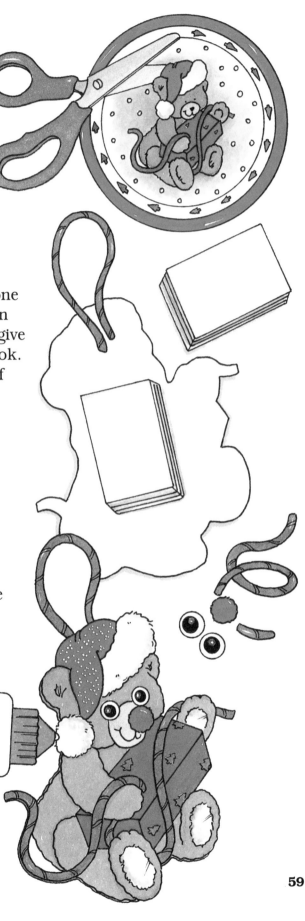

59

Crisscross Ornament

Crisscross ornaments are dramatic decorations for your tree.

What you need:

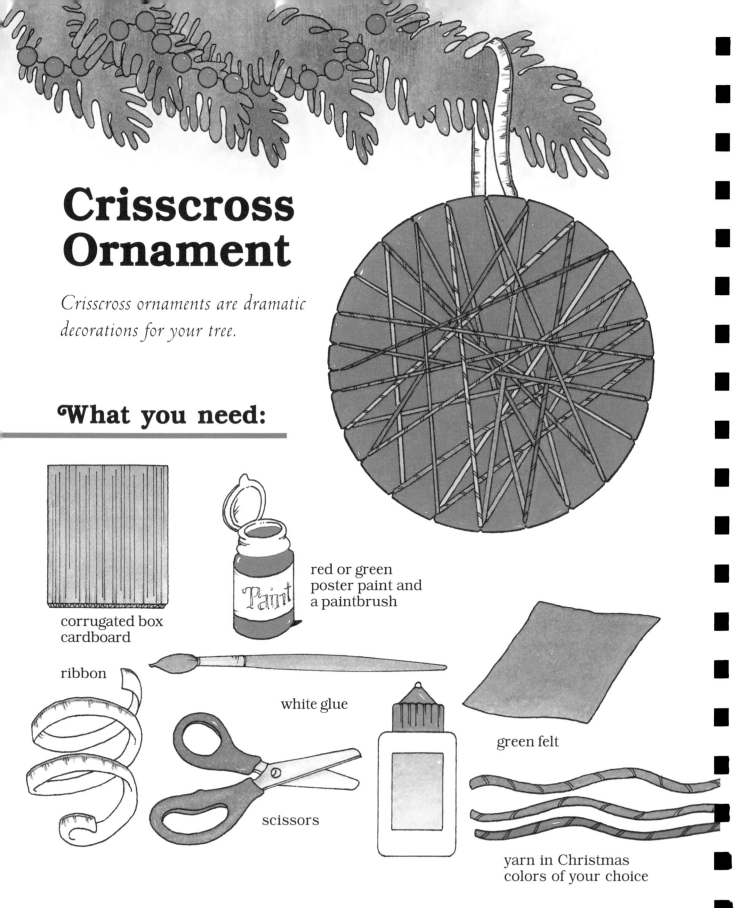

corrugated box cardboard

red or green poster paint and a paintbrush

ribbon

white glue

green felt

scissors

yarn in Christmas colors of your choice

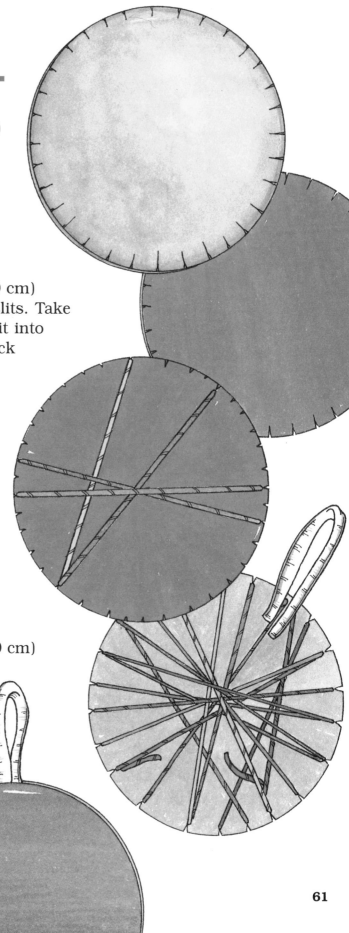

What you do:

1 Cut a 4-inch (10-cm) circle from the cardboard. Cut ½-inch (1½-cm) slits all the way around the edge of the circle and about ¼ to ½ inch (½ to 1¼ cm) apart.

2 Paint the front of the circle and let it dry.

3 Cut a piece of yarn at least 2 feet (60 cm) long. Slide one end into one of the slits. Take the yarn across the circle and slide it into another slit. Crisscross the yarn back and forth over the circle in all different angles to cover the circle with lines of yarn. When the yarn you have cut runs out, start a new piece in a different color. Keep crisscrossing the circle with different colors of yarn until you like the way it looks.

4 Cut a 4-inch (10-cm) piece of ribbon. Glue the two ends of the ribbon to the back of the circle to form a hanger.

5 Cut a circle of green felt 4 inches (10 cm) wide. Glue the circle to the back of the ornament to finish it.

Try lots of different color combinations of paint and yarn. You might want to add some gold trim or thin ribbon to your ornament.

Pipe Cleaner Reindeer

This reindeer is so easy, you can make one for each of your friends in no time at all.

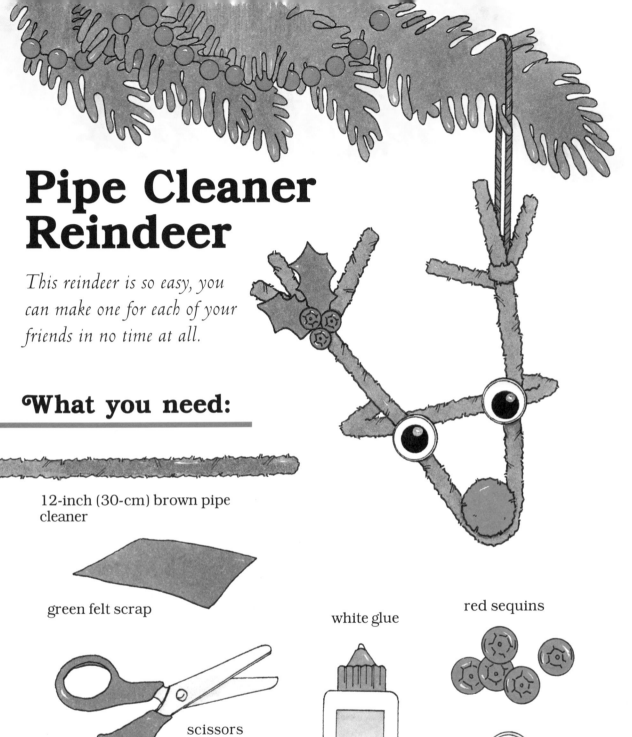

What you need:

12-inch (30-cm) brown pipe cleaner

green felt scrap

scissors

white glue

red sequins

two wiggle eyes

red pom-pom

red embroidery floss

What you do:

1 Cut a 6-inch (15-cm) piece of brown pipe cleaner. Fold the pipe cleaner in half to form a V shape.

2 Cut a second piece of pipe cleaner about 2½ inches (6 cm) long. Set the piece across the V shape about one third of the way up. Wrap the pipe cleaner once around both branches of the V. Fold the leftover ends of the second pipe cleaner back to form ears for the reindeer.

3 Cut the remaining piece of pipe cleaner in half. Wrap a piece around the top portion of each side of the V to make antler prongs for the reindeer.

4 Glue a wiggle eye on each side of the V below the ears. Glue the pom-pom nose on the point of the V.

5 Cut two holly leaves from the green felt. Glue the leaves on one antler. Glue some red sequin berries between the two leaves. Cut an 8-inch (20-cm) piece of embroidery floss. Tie it around the antler without the holly on it. Make a knot in the end of the floss to form a hanger loop.

Pipe cleaner reindeer also make very nice package decorations.

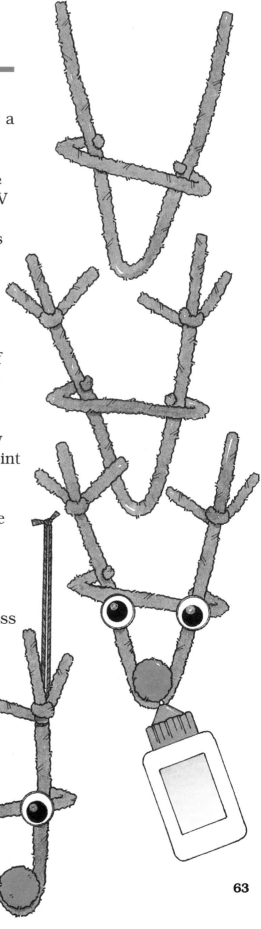

Napkin-Covered Balls

*Use this idea to make beautiful
Christmas tree balls.*

What you need:

Christmas napkin with
colorful figure or pattern

white glue

clear glitter

scissors

newspaper
to work on

2½-inch
(1½-cm)
Styrofoam
ball

paintbrush

pipe cleaner

margarine tub
for mixing

Styrofoam egg carton
for drying

What you do:

1 Choose the part of the napkin that you wish to be on the front of your ornament. Center your main design on the ball and wrap the napkin around the ball to completely cover it. Trim off most of the excess napkin. Remove the napkin from the ball.

2 Mix one part water to three parts glue in the margarine tub. Roll the ball in the tub to completely cover it with the watery glue.

3 Carefully wrap the trimmed napkin around the wet ball to cover it.

4 Cut a 3-inch (7-cm) piece of pipe cleaner. Push the two ends into the top of the ball to make a hanger for the ornament.

5 Hold the ornament by the hanger and use the paintbrush to cover the outside of the ball with the watery glue. Sprinkle the entire ball with clear glitter. Let it dry completely in a Styrofoam egg carton. (This will allow it to dry with most of the surface of the ornament exposed to the air.)

Original ornaments are only as limited as your supply of different holiday napkins!

Feed the Birds Ornament

This ornament would make a great gift for someone who is especially fond of birds.

♥What you need:

four 12-inch (30-cm) brown pipe cleaners

large flat button

masking tape

stickers or pictures of winter birds from old greeting cards

birdseed

white glue

scissors

gold thread

fiberfill

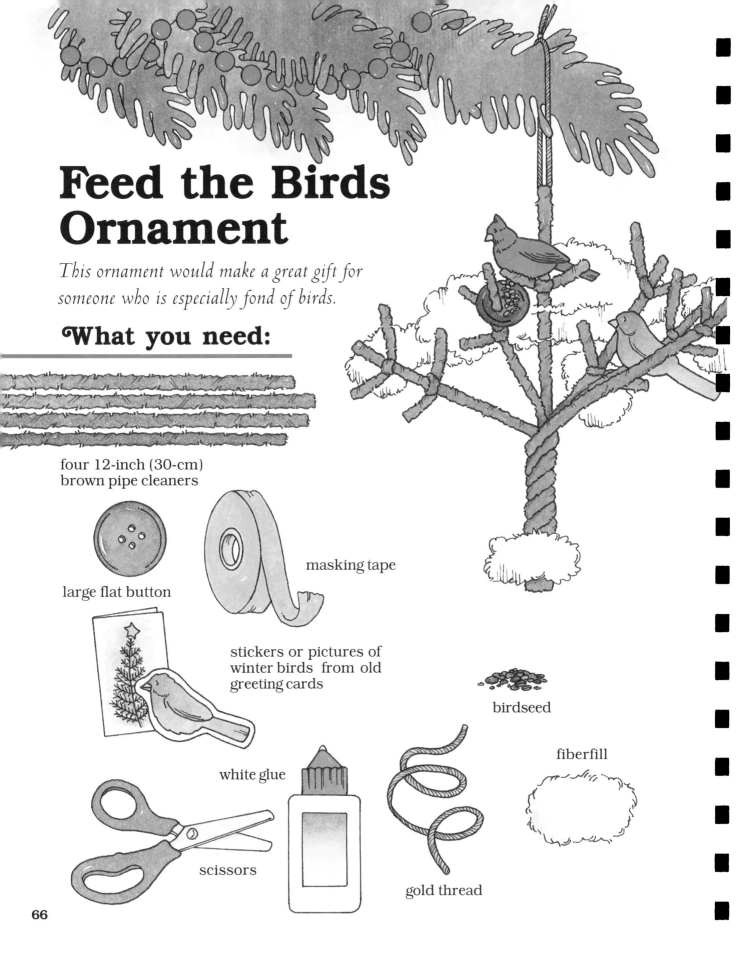

What you do:

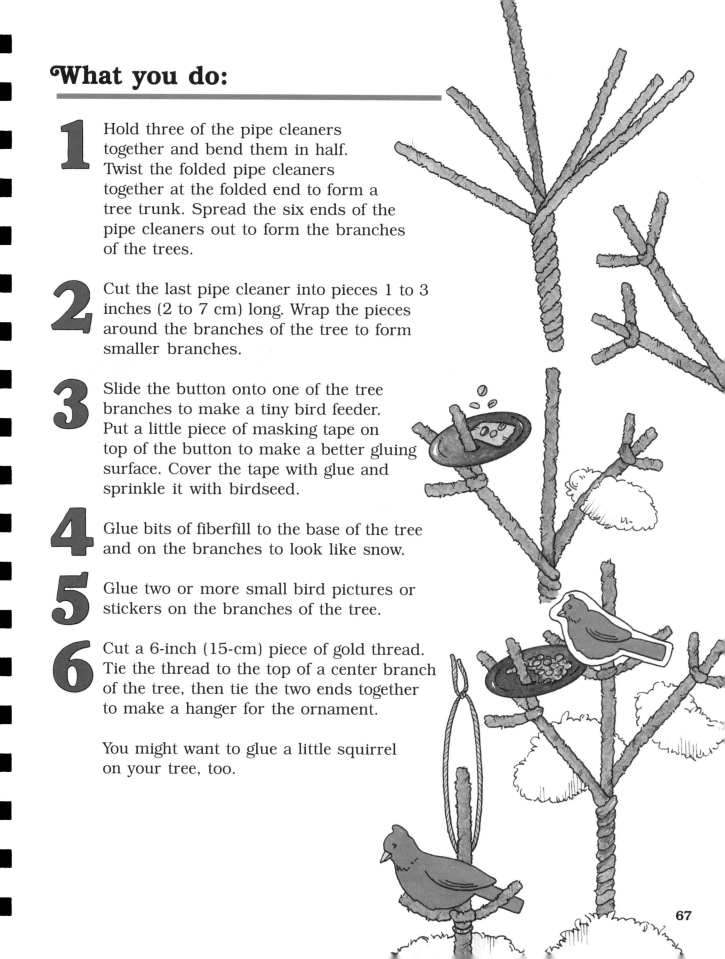

1 Hold three of the pipe cleaners together and bend them in half. Twist the folded pipe cleaners together at the folded end to form a tree trunk. Spread the six ends of the pipe cleaners out to form the branches of the trees.

2 Cut the last pipe cleaner into pieces 1 to 3 inches (2 to 7 cm) long. Wrap the pieces around the branches of the tree to form smaller branches.

3 Slide the button onto one of the tree branches to make a tiny bird feeder. Put a little piece of masking tape on top of the button to make a better gluing surface. Cover the tape with glue and sprinkle it with birdseed.

4 Glue bits of fiberfill to the base of the tree and on the branches to look like snow.

5 Glue two or more small bird pictures or stickers on the branches of the tree.

6 Cut a 6-inch (15-cm) piece of gold thread. Tie the thread to the top of a center branch of the tree, then tie the two ends together to make a hanger for the ornament.

You might want to glue a little squirrel on your tree, too.

Dog Biscuit Doggie

If you make this doggie ornament for your favorite pooch, you'd better hang it up high or it might disappear!

What you need:

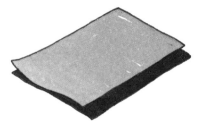

green and black felt scraps

two wiggle eyes

thin red ribbon

blue glue gel

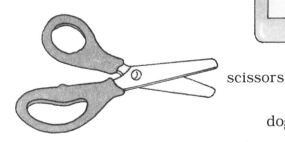

scissors

dog biscuit

brown pom-pom

red sequin

What you do:

1 Cut a pair of floppy ears from the black felt. Glue the ears hanging down from one end of the front of the dog biscuit.

2 Glue on two wiggle eyes below the ears.

3 Glue the pom-pom nose to the other end of the biscuit.

4 Cut two holly leaves from the green felt. Glue the leaves between the ears of the dog. Glue a sequin berry in the center of the leaves.

5 Cut a 6-inch (15-cm) piece of ribbon. Glue the two ends of the ribbon to the back of the biscuit to make a hanger.

Woof, woof! That's dog talk for "Merry Christmas!"

Reindeer Treat Holder

Use an old party hat to make a container for candy and other small surprises.

What you need:

red or green poster paint and a paintbrush

old party hat

two large wiggle eyes

stapler

scissors

red felt scrap

large red pom-pom

two 12-inch (30-cm) red pipe cleaners

glue

red tissue paper

What you do:

1 If the party hat is not a solid color or is not the color you want, paint the outside of the hat red or green.

2 Turn the hat upside-down to form a container with an elastic handle.

3 Cut one of the red pipe cleaners in half. Staple one piece of the pipe cleaner to each side of the hat where the elastic is attached. These will be the antlers. Cut two 5-inch (13-cm) pieces from the second pipe cleaner. Wrap a piece around each antler to form the branches of the antlers.

4 Cut two ears from the red felt scrap. Glue them below the antlers.

5 Glue the two wiggle eyes about one third of the way down the hat.

6 Glue the red pom-pom nose on the front of the point of the hat.

Tuck a square of tissue inside the hat to hold some candies or other treats. One of these ornaments would make a nice gift for a friend.

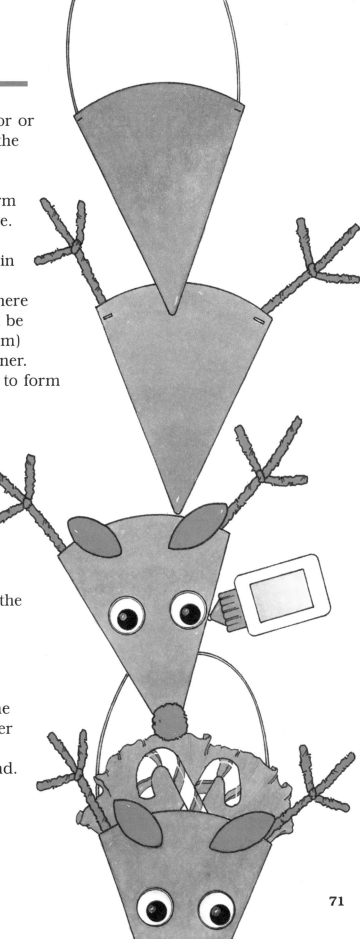

71

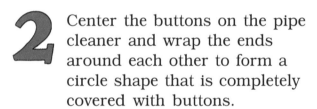

Shank Button Wreath

Shank buttons, the ones with a small loop on the back, make beautiful wreath ornaments.

What you need:

nine shank buttons

12-inch (30-cm) green pipe cleaner

scissors

thin green ribbon

What you do:

1 Thread all of the buttons onto the pipe cleaner so that they are touching each other.

2 Center the buttons on the pipe cleaner and wrap the ends around each other to form a circle shape that is completely covered with buttons.

3 Use the excess pipe cleaner to form a small circle hanger at the top of the wreath. Trim off any extra pipe cleaner that you do not need.

4 Tie the green ribbon in a bow around the base of the hanger.

A collection of all different metal shank buttons makes an especially beautiful wreath ornament.

Bead and Bell Ornament

Many different looks can be achieved with this ornament by using beads of different colors and shapes.

What you need:

12-inch (30-cm) pipe cleaner

large jingle bell   small beads

What you do:

1 Fold the pipe cleaner in half. String the bell onto the pipe cleaner so that it hangs down from the fold.

2 String one bead over both pipe cleaners and slide it down to the bell. Next string

a bead on each pipe cleaner stem and slide them down until they are next to each other. Use any combination of these two methods to string the beads on the pipe cleaner.

3 Leave a 1½-inch (4-cm) piece of pipe cleaner on each side of the top of the ornament. Twist the two ends together to make a hanger for the ornament.

You might want to try stringing buttons or pasta instead of beads.

Handprint Reindeer

The little reindeer will remind you of just what size your hand was the Christmas you made it.

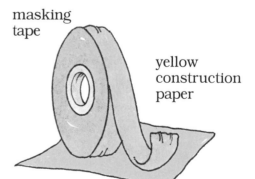

What you need:

wiggle eye

red and brown poster paint and a paintbrush

red string or yarn

masking tape

white glue

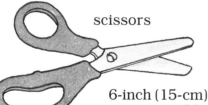
scissors

6-inch (15-cm) green sparkle stem or pipe cleaner

yellow construction paper

What you do:

1 Hold your hand palm-up. Paint the tip of your thumb red. Paint the rest of your thumb, hand, and fingers brown.

2 Spread your thumb and fingers apart and make a handprint on the yellow paper.

3 When the paint has dried, cut out the handprint.

4 Your thumb is the head of the reindeer with a red nose. Glue a wiggle eye on the brown part of the thumb.

5 Cut a 4½-inch (1½-cm) piece from the pipe cleaner and fold it in half to make two antlers. Cut the remaining pipe cleaner in half. Wrap a piece around each antler to make the branches of the antler.

6 Glue the fold of the pipe cleaner behind the head of the reindeer so that the antlers stick out above the head. Use the masking tape to hold them in place while the glue dries.

7 Cut a 6-inch (15-cm) piece of red string. Tie the two ends together to make a loop. Glue the knot of the loop behind the reindeer to make a hanger for the ornament.

Write your name and the date on the back of the reindeer and give it to a special grown-up.

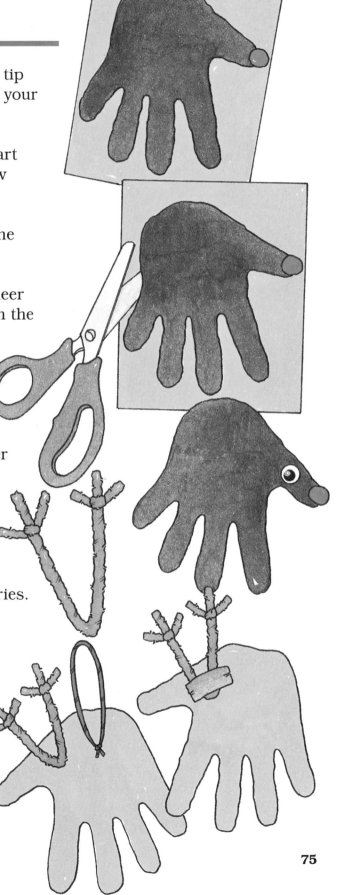

Tray of Cookies Ornament

Everyone likes Christmas cookies!

What you need:

corrugated
box cardboard

masking
tape

aluminum foil

white glue

scissors

red felt

one or more
different
color glues

shape punches such as star,
teddy bear, and Christmas
tree

thin red
ribbon

brown construction
paper scraps

What you do:

1 Cut a rectangle from the cardboard about 2½ inches (6 cm) by 3½ inches (9 cm). Cover the cardboard with aluminum foil to make it look like a cookie sheet.

2 Cut a 6-inch (15-cm) piece of ribbon. Tape the two ends to the back of one corner of the cookie sheet to make a hanger.

3 Cover the back of the cookie sheet with masking tape to create a better gluing surface.

4 Cut a 2½-inch (6-cm) by 3½-inch (9-cm) rectangle of felt and glue it to the back of the cookie sheet.

5 Use the shape punches to cut little cookies from the brown paper.

6 Put a tiny piece of masking tape over each place on the cookie sheet you want to put a cookie. Glue a cookie on each piece of tape.

7 Use the colored glues to "frost" the cookies.

This little ornament looks so yummy that you'll want to make some real Christmas cookies to eat.

Peaceful Dove

*Fly this beautiful bird among
the branches of your tree.*

What you need:

three round
coffee filters

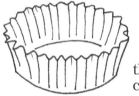

sharp black marker

thin red
ribbon

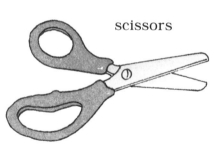

white glue

scissors

clamp clothespin

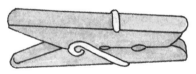

Styrofoam tray
for drying

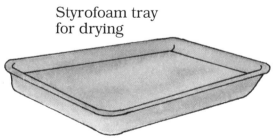

6-inch (15-cm) green pipe
cleaner

What you do:

1 Fold one coffee filter into quarters for the tail of the dove. Glue the tail to one side of the back handle half of the clothespin, with the pleated end sticking out past the clothespin.

2 Fold the next filter into eighths for the head of the dove. Use the marker to draw an eye on each side of the head, and a beak. Glue the head to the front part of the same side of the clothespin as the tail, with the point sticking out beyond the front of the clothespin.

3 Fold the last filter in half with glue between the folds to hold it in place. This will be the wings. Glue the wings over the top of the clothespin so that the end of the tail sticks out from the pleated end of the wings and the pointed head sticks out from the flat side of the wings.

4 Shape a wreath 1½ inches (4 cm) wide from the green pipe cleaner by wrapping the pipe cleaner around and around itself in a circle.

5 Tie a tiny bow from the red ribbon. Glue the bow to the wreath.

6 Slip the beak of the dove between the layers of the wreath. Hold the wreath in place with a drop of glue.

Attach the dove to your tree by clamping it to a branch with the clothespin underneath it.

Foil Ring Ornament

This decoration is so easy you might want to try making it with a younger brother or sister.

What you need:

cardboard toilet-tissue tube

scissors

aluminum foil

red yarn

tiny Christmas ball

hole punch

What you do:

1 Cut a 1-inch (2½-cm) band from the end of the cardboard tube.

2 Cover the band both inside and out with aluminum foil.

3 Punch a hole in the band.

4 Cut an 8-inch (20-cm) piece of red yarn. String the colored ball onto the yarn.

5 String the ends of the yarn through the hole from the inside of the tube to the outside so that the ball hangs down inside the band. Tie the two ends of the yarn together to make a hanger.

This ornament looks so pretty reflecting the lights on the tree. Try making some using jingle bells instead of the Christmas balls.

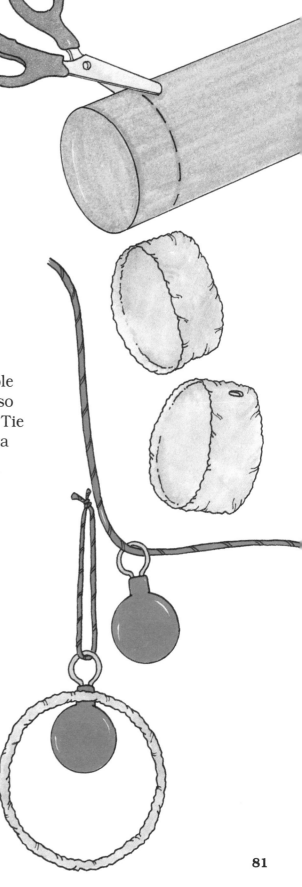

Circle Garland

Make this garland to drape around your tree.

What you need:

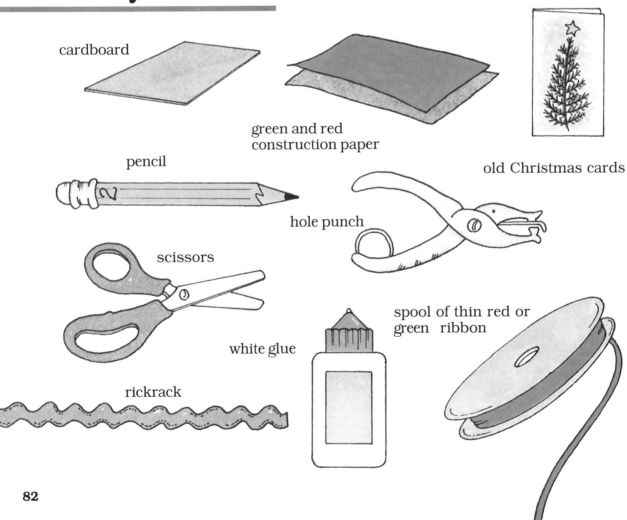

cardboard

green and red
construction paper

old Christmas cards

pencil

hole punch

scissors

white glue

spool of thin red or
green ribbon

rickrack

What you do:

1 Make a 2-inch (5-cm) circle pattern from the cardboard.

2 Use the pattern to cut out lots of circles from the construction paper. Punch two holes, about 1 inch (2½ cm) apart near the edge of each circle. This will be the top of the circle. Decorate each circle with rickrack.

3 Use the pattern to cut out picture circles from old Christmas cards. Make as many picture circles as you made construction paper circles. Punch two holes in the top of each circle.

4 Cut a piece of ribbon long enough to string all your circles on. Alternate picture circles and construction paper circles on the ribbon, threading the ribbon through the back of each hole, then down through the front of the second hole.

5 Tie off each end of the garland and wrap it around the branches of your tree.

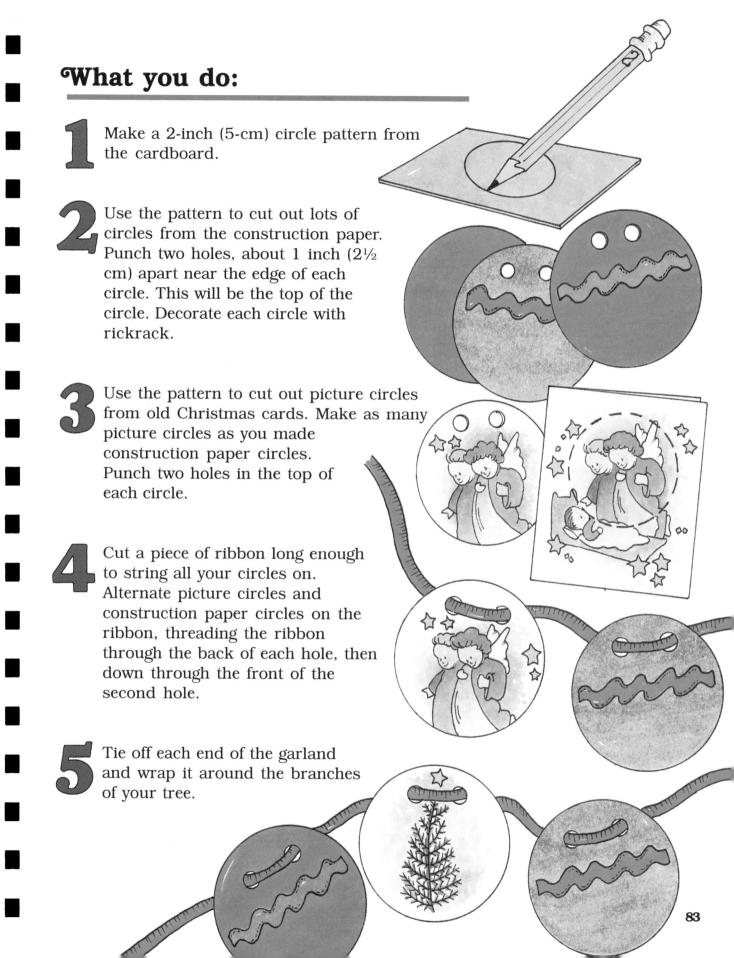

Spaghetti Wreath

Did you ever think that spaghetti could turn into a pine wreath?

What you need:

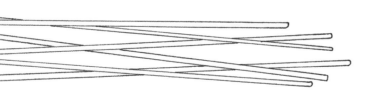

uncooked spaghetti

white glue

red
nail polish

green
food
coloring

margarine tub
with lid

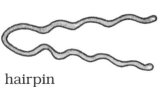

hairpin

one piece of
bow-tie pasta

craft stick

What you do:

1 Break spaghetti into ¼- to ½-inch (½- to 1-cm) pieces to get about ½ cup of spaghetti bits.

2 Use the craft stick to mix about ½ cup of glue with a few drops of green food coloring in the margarine tub.

3 Add the spaghetti bits to the glue and mix until the spaghetti is completely coated with green glue.

4 Shape the gluey spaghetti on the plastic lid in the shape of a 2½-inch (1½-cm) wreath. This ornament is best kept small because the pasta is quite heavy.

5 Slip a hairpin into one edge of the wreath to make a hanger.

6 Paint the bow-tie pasta red with the nail polish. Glue the red bow on the wreath.

When the wreath is completely dry, peel it off the plastic lid. It will take at least a day and maybe longer to dry.

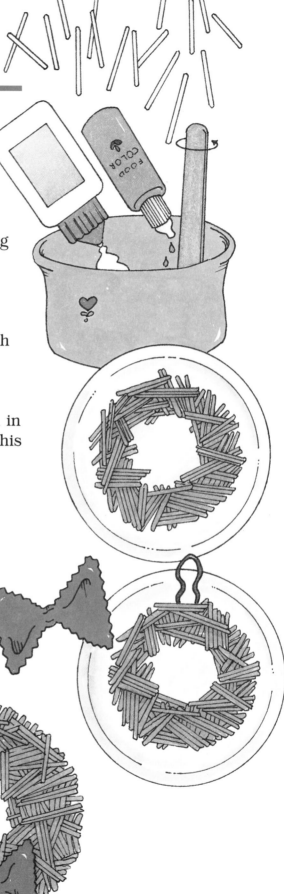

Gingerbread Cookie Ornament

This cookie ornament smells good enough to eat!

What you need:

corrugated box cardboard

sequins

scissors

white glue

gingerbread person cookie cutter

cinnamon

tiny red pom-pom

pencil

thin red ribbon

red rickrack

Styrofoam tray to work on

What you do:

1 Trace around the cookie cutter on the cardboard. Cut out the gingerbread person shape.

2 Cover the shape with glue, then sprinkle it with cinnamon. Let the glue dry completely, then shake off any excess cinnamon.

3 Use the sequins to give the cookie person eyes and buttons. Glue on the pom-pom for a nose. Cut a tiny smile from the rickrack and glue it in place. Use strips of rickrack to decorate the head, arms, and legs.

4 Cut a 5-inch (13-cm) strip of ribbon. Glue the two ends of the ribbon to the back of the head of the gingerbread person to make a hanger for the ornament.

Do you smell freshly-baked cookies?

Christmas Bell

This little bell ornament really rings.

What you need:

paper napkin with Christmas pattern all over it

1½-inch (4-cm) Styrofoam ball

jingle bell

thin red ribbon

scissors

bowl and spoon for mixing

newspaper to work on

white glue

bathroom-size paper cup

Styrofoam tray for drying

red pipe cleaner

What you do:

1 Ask a grown-up to cut the Styrofoam ball in half for you.

2 Cut a 6-inch (15-cm) piece of ribbon. Thread the jingle bell onto the ribbon. Poke a hole in the bottom of the cup. Holding the cup upside down, thread the two ends of the ribbon up through the inside of the cup and through the hole so that the bell hangs down slightly below the rim of the cup.

3 Rub glue over the outer bottom of the cup and the ends of the ribbon. Stick the flat side of the Styrofoam ball over the bottom of the cup and the ribbon ends.

4 Mix about ½ cup of glue with a few drops of water. Open the napkin and gently swish it around in the glue to completely cover it. If you have a large napkin, you may want to cut it down first. You will need enough to cover the outside of the bell.

5 Drape the gluey napkin over the cup bell, shaping it to the cup. Trim off the extra napkin at the bottom.

6 Cut a 3-inch (8-cm) piece of pipe cleaner. Push the two ends of the pipe cleaner into the Styrofoam top of the bell to make a hanger.

Jingle bells, jingle bells...

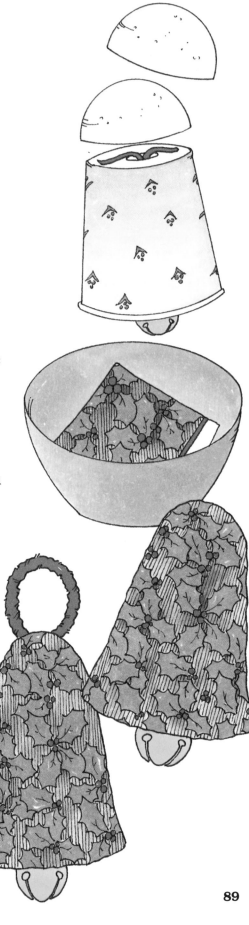

89

Wooden Spoon Snowman

Make this cold-weather friend from an old ice-cream spoon.

What you need:

wooden ice-cream spoon

scissors

white glue

black, orange, and red felt scraps

Styrofoam tray for drying

string

white poster paint with paintbrush

What you do:

1 Paint the ice-cream spoon white and let it dry.

2 The smaller, handle end of the spoon will be the head of the snowman. Cut out a hat, eyes, and buttons from the black felt and glue them in place. Cut a carrot nose from the orange felt and a scarf from the red felt and glue them on the snowman.

3 Cut a 5-inch (13-cm) piece of string. Glue the two ends between the snowman's hat and the spoon to make a hanger for the ornament.

This little fellow won't melt at the end of the season.

If you add a safety pin to his hat instead of the hanger, you can wear him as a pin.

Hands and Foot Angel

Turn your hands and foot shapes into a little angel.

What you need:

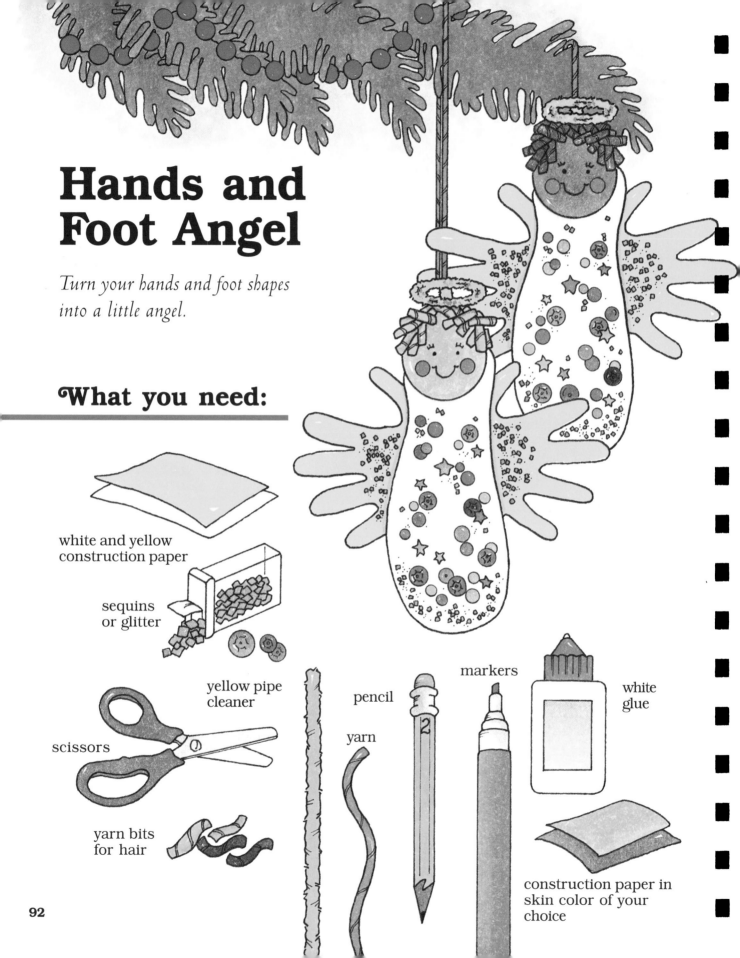

white and yellow construction paper

sequins or glitter

scissors

yellow pipe cleaner

yarn bits for hair

yarn

pencil

markers

white glue

construction paper in skin color of your choice

What you do:

1 Trace around your bare foot on the white paper. Cut out the foot shape for the body of the angel.

2 Trace around your hands on the yellow paper. Cut out the hand shapes for the wings of the angel. Glue the wings sticking out from each side of the middle portion of the foot.

3 Cut a 2-inch (5-cm) circle from the skin-color construction paper for the head of the angel. Glue the head to the heel end of the foot shape on the opposite side that the wings are glued on.

4 Shape a halo from the yellow pipe cleaner. Trim the end of the halo to about 2 inches (5 cm) long. Dip the end in glue and slip it between the top of the head and the body of the angel.

5 Cut a 5-inch (13-cm) piece of yarn. Tie the yarn around the halo, then tie the two ends together to make a hanger for the angel.

6 Use the markers to draw a face on the head of the angel. Cut yarn bits and glue them around the face for hair.

7 Decorate the halo, body, and wings of the angel with glitter and sequins.

Give the little angel to someone to remind them of another little angel . . . you, of course!

Tube Reindeer

This reindeer is so easy that you can make enough to pull Santa's sleigh in no time at all.

What you need:

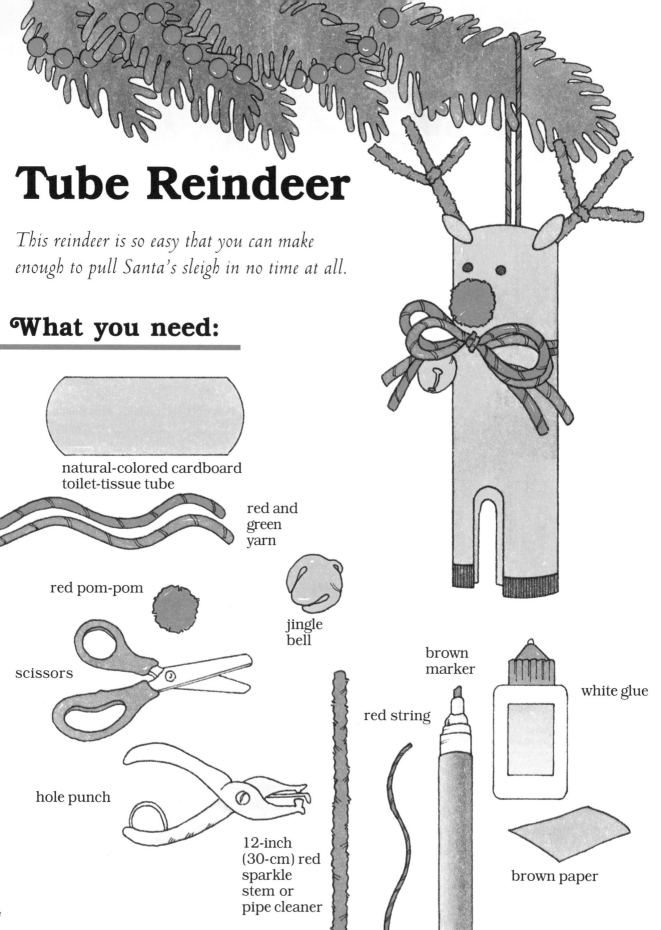

natural-colored cardboard toilet-tissue tube

red and green yarn

red pom-pom

scissors

jingle bell

hole punch

12-inch (30-cm) red sparkle stem or pipe cleaner

red string

brown marker

white glue

brown paper

1 Cut four rectangles from the bottom edge of the tube that are 1½ inches (4 cm) high and ¼ inch (0.6 cm) wide and spaced equal distance apart around the edge of the tube. This will leave four pieces of tube hanging down for the reindeer legs. Color a brown hoof on the bottom of each leg.

2 Punch a hole in each side of the edge at the top of the tube. Cut the sparkle stem in half. Thread one half through the two holes, then bend each end up to form antlers. Cut the second piece of sparkle stem in half and wrap a piece around each antler to form the branches of the antlers.

3 Cut two ears for the reindeer from the brown paper. Glue them on the head below the antlers.

4 Draw two eyes with the brown marker. Glue on a red pom-pom for the nose.

5 Cut 8-inch (20-cm) pieces of red yarn and green yarn. Tie the two pieces of yarn around the neck of the reindeer and tie them in a knot. Thread the jingle bell onto one of the pieces of yarn and slide it down to the knot. Tie the yarn in a bow with the jingle bell hanging down from the bow.

6 Cut a 5-inch (13-cm) piece of string. Punch a hole in the back of the head of the reindeer. Thread the string through the hole and tie the two ends together to make a hanger for the ornament.

Hang the reindeer on the tree quickly, before it flies away!

Christmas Stocking

Use the fingers from an old knit glove to make miniature Christmas stockings.

What you need:

old knit glove

two tiny
wiggle eyes

fiberfill

rickrack

white glue

scissors

red and white pipe cleaners

small
pom-pom

three tiny
pom-poms

What you do:

1 Cut a finger from the glove to use as the stocking. Stuff the finger with fiberfill, pushing the stuffing in the fingertip over to one side to resemble the foot of a stocking.

2 Cut a 2-inch (5-cm) piece from both the red and the white pipe cleaners. Twist the two different colors together to make a little candy cane. Dip the end of the candy cane in glue and slide it down in one side of the stocking, between the fiberfill and the stocking.

3 Make a tiny teddy bear to peek out of the other side of the stocking. For its head, glue the small pom-pom on top of the fiberfill next to the candy cane. Glue on two tiny pom-pom ears, two tiny eyes, and a pom-pom nose.

4 Glue fiberfill around the top rim of the stocking. Decorate around the fiberfill with rickrack.

5 Cut a 3-inch (8-cm) piece of pipe cleaner. Tuck the two ends down into the stocking behind the teddy bear to make a hanger for the ornament.

This little stocking looks like a Christmas surprise for a mouse!

Berry Basket Snowflakes

Make a snowman's favorite ornament.

What you need:

plastic berry basket

clear glitter

plastic bowl for mixing

white glue

Styrofoam tray to work on

paintbrush

water

scissors

green yarn

facial tissue

What you do:

1 Cut the sides out of the basket. Cut three branched stems from the side and bottom of the basket.

2 Mix about ¼ cup of white glue with a small amount of water to thin it enough to paint the delicate tissue.

3 Spread the tissue out on the Styrofoam tray. Paint the tissue carefully with the watery glue. Arrange the three berry basket stems on top of the tissue, crisscrossing them to make a snowflake.

4 Cover the snowflake with another tissue. Dab the top tissue with more glue to completely cover the snowflake and the area around the snowflake.

5 Sprinkle the snowflake with the clear glitter. Let the project dry overnight.

6 When the tissue has dried completely, peel it off the tray. Trim away the excess tissue around the outside of the snowflake.

7 Cut a 5-inch (13-cm) piece of yarn. Tie the two ends together to make a hanger. Glue the hanger along the back of the snowflake with the loop sticking up from the top.

It is important to glue the hanger straight along the stem of one of the snowflake arms so that the ornament will hang straight.

Poinsettia Ornament

The poinsettia is a traditional plant of the Christmas season.

What you need:

cardboard egg carton

gold sequins

scissors

Styrofoam tray to work on

gold thread

white glue

red and green poster paint and a paintbrush

What you do:

1 Cut two cups from the egg carton. Cut five points around the edge of one of the cups for the red top of the plant. Cut four points around the edge of the second cup for the green leaves underneath.

2 Paint the five-point cup red. Paint the four-point cup green. Gently open the damp points partway and let them dry.

3 Cut a 5-inch (13-cm) piece of gold thread. Glue the red cup over the green cup with the ends of the thread in between them to make a hanger for the ornament.

4 Make a center for the flower by gluing several gold sequins in the middle of the red cup.

You can make just one poinsettia to hang or make three of them to glue together in a cluster for a larger ornament.

Photo Locket Ornament

*Hang a picture of you on
the Christmas tree!*

What you need:

two identical small lids, such as from baby-food jars

red nail polish

white glue

scissors

a small photo of you

green ribbon

red and green rickrack

plastic lid for drying

green sticker stars

masking tape

green construction paper scrap and red felt scrap

What you do:

1 Paint both lids outside and around the inner edges with the red nail polish. Let the lids dry on the plastic lid.

2 Cut a 3- by ½-inch (8- by 1½-cm) rectangle of felt for a hinge between the two lids. Cover the inside of each lid with masking tape to create a better gluing surface. Glue one end of the hinge inside each lid.

3 Trace around the lid on the construction paper. Cut out the circle and trim it to fit inside one lid. Center the circle over the image you want to show on your photo and trace around it. Cut out the photo.

4 Cover the ends of the hinges with masking tape. Glue the circle of construction paper in the top lid and a photo inside the bottom lid.

5 Decorate the outside of both lids with the rickrack and stars.

6 Cut a 5-inch (13-cm) piece of ribbon. Tie the ribbon around the felt hinge between the two lids, then tie the ends together to make a hanger for the ornament.

Photo lockets make a nice Christmas surprise for someone special in your life. You could use two photos and make a gift from you and your brother or sister.

Paper Filter Angel

Fly an angel among the branches of your tree.

What you need:

round, white coffee filter

¾-inch (2-cm) wooden craft bead

white glue

two wiggle eyes

scissors

two white craft feathers

gold sparkle stem

gold thread

yarn for hair

red thread

gold stars

What you do:

1 To make the dress, fold the filter down around itself and twist the center. Dip the twist in glue and stick it in the hole in the bead, which will be the head of the angel.

2 Cut a 3-inch (8-cm) piece of sparkle stem. Shape the stem into a halo and slip the end into the hole at the top of the head. Squeeze a drop of glue in the hole to secure the halo.

3 Cut a 4-inch (10-cm) piece of gold thread. Slide the two ends down in the gluey hole with the halo to make a hanger for the ornament.

4 Cut yarn bits and glue them on the head for hair. Glue on the two wiggle eyes. Cut a tiny piece of red thread and glue it on the face in the shape of a smile.

5 Glue the two feathers sticking out from the back of the angel for wings.

6 Decorate the angel's dress with gold stars.

You might want to add other decorations to the angel's dress such as sequins or glitter.

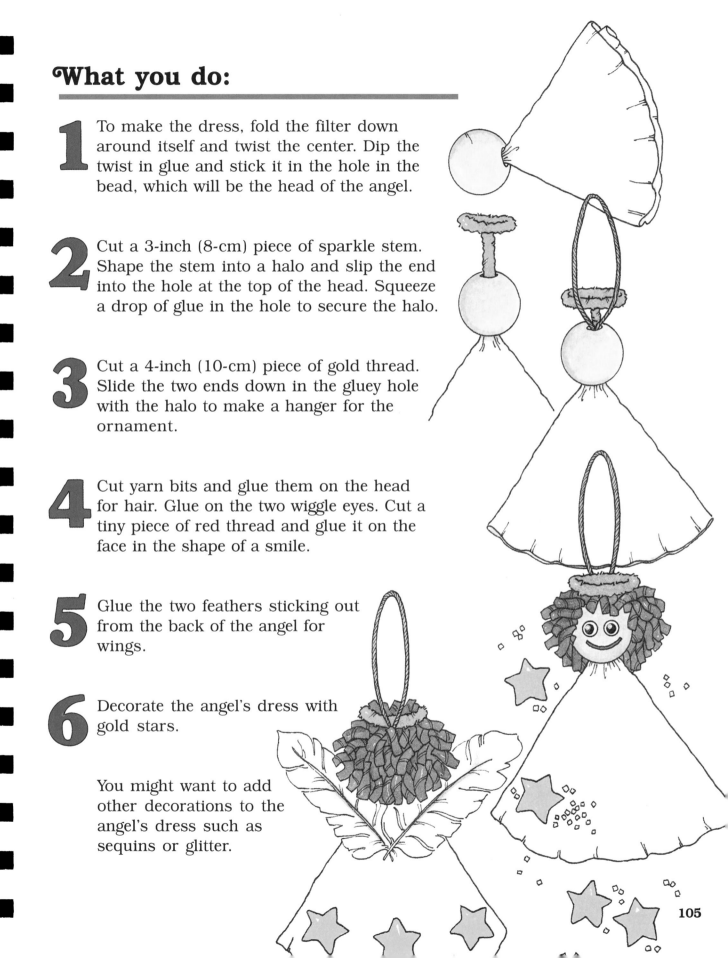

Shoulder Pad Angel

This charming angel is for the very top of your Christmas tree.

What you need:

pair of oval shoulder pads in a pretty Christmas color or print

pink poster paint and a paintbrush

pair of white shoulder pads

silver sparkle stem

6-inch (15-cm) white pipe cleaner

yellow yarn

thin ribbon

white glue

two wiggle eyes

scissors

2-inch (5-cm) Styrofoam ball

large sequins in red and purple

stapler

Styrofoam tray for drying

What you do:

1 Push the pipe cleaner into the Styrofoam ball to make a neck for the angel. Paint the ball pink for the head and let it dry on the Styrofoam tray.

2 Shape a small halo for the angel from the sparkle stem. Push the end of the halo into the top of the head.

3 Cut the yellow yarn into tiny pieces of hair. Glue the hair onto the head around the halo.

4 Glue on two wiggle eyes and a red sequin mouth. Glue on two purple sequin cheeks.

5 To make the dress of the angel, staple the two oval shoulder pads together with the puffed side facing out on each side and the neck of the angel between them at the pointed end of the shoulder pads. Do not staple the bottom of the dress together as this is how the angel will slip over the top of the tree.

6 Fold each of the white shoulder pads in half to make wings. Hold the folds with staples. Staple the wings to the back of the angel.

7 Tie a bow from the ribbon and glue it to the front neck of the angel.

You might want to add other decorations to your angel's dress and wings, such as glitter, metallic trim, or sequins. Or make a "country" angel and decorate it with lots of buttons.

107

Teddy Bear Present

Turn a flip-top toothpaste cap into a cute little Christmas surprise package.

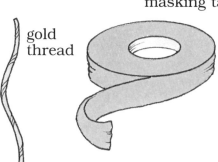

What you need:

flip-top
toothpaste cap

red nail
polish

red and
green thin
ribbon

small pom-pom

two tiny
pom-poms

two tiny
wiggle eyes

green
paper
scrap

sharp
black
marker

blue glue gel

scissors

gold
thread

masking tape

What you do:

1 Open the toothpaste flip top and paint it with red nail polish.

2 Cut a 4-inch (10-cm) piece of gold thread. Thread it through the hinge of the cap and tie the two ends together to make a hanger.

3 Put a tiny piece of masking tape over the small opening of the cap to create a better gluing surface. Glue the small pom-pom on the tape for a teddy bear head. Glue the two tiny pom-poms on top of the head for ears. Glue the wiggle eyes to the front of the pom-pom.

4 Make a tiny bow from the red ribbon. Glue the bow at the neck of the teddy bear.

5 Make a small bow from the green ribbon. Put a piece of masking tape on the top of the cap, then glue the bow on the masking tape.

6 Make a tiny tag from the green paper. Write a Christmas message on it with the marker, and slip it, face down, under the bow so that it sticks out behind the bear.

This ornament is small enough to look nice on a little tabletop Christmas tree.

Cut Tube Decoration

You can make one of these decorated tubes to hang as an ornament or make lots of them to tie together as a garland to wrap around your tree.

What you need:

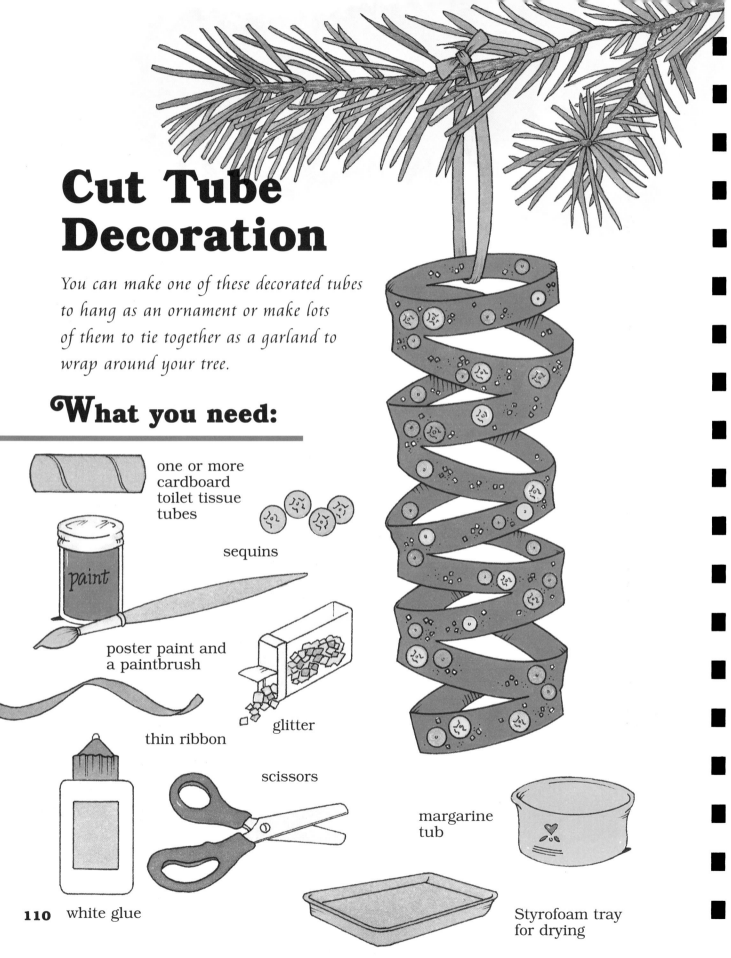

one or more cardboard toilet tissue tubes

sequins

poster paint and a paintbrush

glitter

thin ribbon

scissors

margarine tub

white glue

Styrofoam tray for drying

What you do:

1 Flatten the cardboard tube. Make a 2-inch (5-cm) cut about ½ inch (1 cm) from the end of the tube. Do not cut the tube apart. Make another 2-inch (5-cm) cut on the opposite side of the tube and about ½ inch (1 cm) beyond the first cut. Continue cutting the entire tube on opposite sides and at ½-inch (1-cm) intervals.

2 Gently pull on the two ends of the tube to spread the cuts apart.

3 Mix four parts paint to one part white glue in the margarine tub. Paint the tube both inside and out.

4 Sprinkle the wet paint with sequins and glitter.

5 Gently pull the wet tube apart again and let it dry on the Styrofoam tray.

6 Thread an 8-inch (20-cm) piece of ribbon through one end of the tube. Tie the two ends together to make a hanger.

If you make several tubes, cut pieces of ribbon to tie the ends together to make a long tube garland.

Bottle Cap Ornament

Need an ornament in a hurry?
Try this one!

What you need:

plastic bottle cap, green if possible

thin red ribbon

large size bubble wrap

sequins or glitter

white glue

scissors

What you do:

1 Cut an 8-inch (20-cm) piece of ribbon. Rub glue around the outside of the bottle cap. Tie the ribbon around the bottle cap, then tie the ends together to make a hanger for the cap.

2 Rub glue over the inside back of the cap. Sprinkle the glue with sequins or glitter.

3 Cut one bubble from the bubble wrap. Rub glue around the inside edges of the cap and slide the bubble wrap into the cap over the sequins.

You might want to try decorating the inside of the cap with a little picture or sticker star with glitter around it.

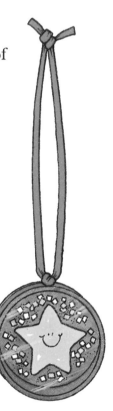
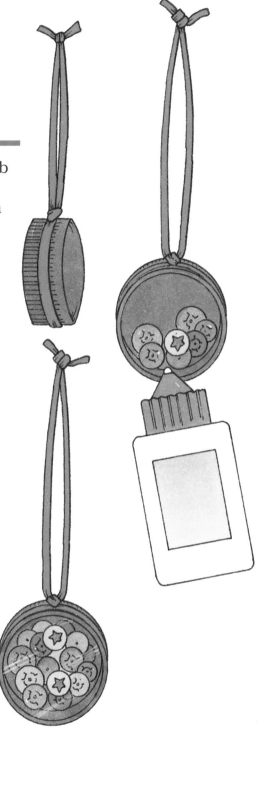

Box Nativity

Make a miniature nativity scene to hang on your tree.

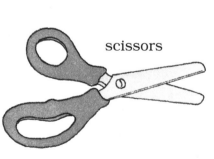

What you need:

old Christmas cards

green ribbon

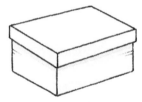
small box with lid (jewelry gift box works well)

sticker star

blue glitter

white glue

scissors

What you do:

1 Tie a piece of green ribbon around the bottom and sides of the bottom of the box. Glue the ribbon in place on the bottom and sides, then tie the two ends together to form a hanger. Stand the bottom of the box on one side in the lid of the box to form a small enclosure with a tray front.

2 Glue the box back into place in the lid.

3 Cover the insides of the box and lid with glue, then sprinkle the glued surface with the blue glitter to cover it.

4 Cut a small picture of the baby Jesus in the manger from an old card. Glue the picture to the back of the box. Cut an animal or a figure such as Mary or Joseph to glue next to the baby if there is room.

5 Cut some animals or figures to stand on the tray part of the box. When you cut the figures, leave a $\frac{1}{2}$-inch (1-cm) tab at the bottom to fold back and glue on the tray so that the figures will stand up.

6 Cut angels or birds to glue to the top edge of the box enclosure. Glue a sticker star in the middle, shining over the baby Jesus.

Each nativity scene you make will be an original, using your own arrangement of figures cut from old cards.

Mylar Tassel

Don't throw away those colorful Mylar balloons that come in balloon bouquets. Save them to make tassels for your Christmas tree.

What you need:

one or more deflated Mylar balloons

thin Mylar package ribbon

large jingle bell

red yarn

scissors

What you do:

1 Cut a rectangle-shaped piece from each side of the balloon about 6 inches (15 cm) tall and as long as the balloon is wide.

2 Fringe the entire length of both rectangles by cutting $^1/_4$-inch ($^1/_2$-cm)-wide strips all the way across, but leaving 1 inch ($2^1/_2$ cm) uncut at the top. The strips may be spiral, which is fine.

3 Stack the two rectangles on top of each other, then roll the uncut top of the fringe around itself as tightly as possible. Tie a piece of ribbon around the rolled top to hold it in place. String the jingle bell onto the ribbon and tie it in place, then tie the ribbon into a bow.

4 Cut a 5-inch (13-cm) piece of yarn. Tie the yarn around the top of the tassel and knot it. Tie the two ends of the yarn together to form a hanger.

No one will ever guess you made your Christmas tassels from balloons saved from birthday and other holiday celebrations during the year.

Paper-Strip Ball Ornament

Choose your own color combination for making this paper-strip ball.

What you need:

construction paper

sequins or glitter

colored tissue paper

gold thread

white glue

scissors

stapler

What you do:

1 Cut three paper strips that are 1 inch (2½ cm) wide and 9 inches (23 cm) long.

2 Arrange the three strips across each other like the spokes of a wheel, with equal space between each spoke. Staple the strips together at the point where they cross.

3 Bring the ends of five of the six strips up to meet to form a ball. Staple the strips to hold them in place.

4 Crumple a square of colored tissue paper and carefully put it inside the ball through the opening left by the strip that has not been attached to the top of the ornament yet.

5 Cut a 5-inch (13-cm) piece of gold thread. Tie the two ends together to make a hanger. Rub glue over the stapled portion at the top of the ball. Set the bottom of the hanger in the glue. Pull the last paper strip up to cover the glue and the bottom part of the hanger.

6 Decorate the paper strips by covering them with glue, then sprinkling them with sequins or glitter.

If you store your paper balls carefully, you will enjoy them for many Christmases to come.

Little Lamb Ornament

This little lamb would look very sweet tucked in among the branches of your tree.

What you need:

6-inch (15-cm) black pipe cleaner

thin red ribbon

gold thread

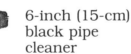
two tiny wiggle eyes

two cotton balls

scissors

white glue

What you do:

1 Cut a 2½-inch (6-cm) piece of black pipe cleaner. Fold about ¼-inch (½-cm) of one end of the pipe cleaner to form a head for the lamb.

2 Cut the remaining piece of pipe cleaner in half. Wrap each piece around the body of the lamb so that the two ends of each piece hang down to form the legs.

3 Rub the body of the lamb with glue, then cover each side with a cotton ball.

4 Cut a 3-inch (8-cm) piece of gold thread. Tie the two ends together to make a hanger.

5 Cut a 5-inch (13-cm) piece of red ribbon. String the ribbon through the hanger, then tie the ribbon around the neck of the lamb. Tie a pretty bow and trim the ends to make it look nice. Slide the hanger around to the opposite side of the bow so that it is at the back of the ornament.

6 Glue the two wiggle eyes on the head of the lamb.

BAA! BAA! You guessed it! That is sheep talk for Merry Christmas!

Glove Reindeer

At last! A great way to recycle knit gloves with missing mates!

What you need:

knit glove

two wiggle eyes

red pom-pom

12-inch (30-cm) red pipe cleaner

red rickrack

thin red ribbon

blue glue gel

scissors

jingle bell

What you do:

1 Cut a 6-inch (15-cm) piece of ribbon. Fold the cuff of the glove into itself and tuck the two ends of the ribbon down between the sides to form a hanger. Glue the two sides together with the ribbon between them.

2 Cut a 6-inch (15-cm) piece from the pipe cleaner. Thread the pipe cleaner through the knit glove about halfway up the thumb. Bend the ends up to form the antlers. Cut the remaining piece of pipe cleaner in half. Wrap a piece around each antler to form the "branches" of the antler.

3 Cut a 6-inch (15-cm) piece of red ribbon. Thread the jingle bell onto the ribbon. Tie the ribbon in a bow around the base of the thumb of the glove with the jingle bell hanging down.

4 Glue a red pom-pom nose on the end of the thumb. Glue the two wiggle eyes on each side of the thumb above the nose.

5 The four fingers of the glove are the reindeer's feet. Cut a piece of rickrack to glue across each foot.

On Dasher, on Dancer . . .

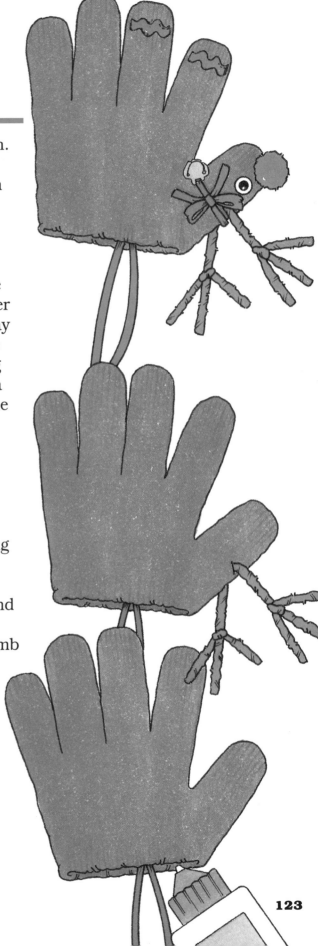

Santa's Helper Ornament

It's a good thing Santa Claus has lots of little elves to help him!

What you need:

construction paper in skin color of your choice

red construction paper scrap

round coffee filter

fiberfill

red pom-pom

red rickrack

thin green ribbon

green marker

white glue

two wiggle eyes

jingle bell

scissors

masking tape

What you do:

1 Fold the coffee filter in half. Fold the half in thirds by folding one side over the other. Glue the folds in place.

2 Cut a 2-inch (5-cm) circle from the skin-colored paper. Cut about one fourth of the circle off on one side. The flattened part of the circle will be the top of the head.

3 To make the hat, color the point of the folded filter green to about a third of the way down.

4 Glue the head on below the hat with the flat part across the bottom of the hat.

5 Glue the wiggle eyes and a pom-pom nose on the face. Cut two cheeks from the red paper and glue them on each side of the face.

6 Glue fiberfill on the bottom portion of the filter for a beard.

7 Glue a band of fiberfill then a band of rickrack across the top of the hat.

8 Put a small piece of masking tape on the base of the bell to create a better gluing surface. Glue the bell to the top of the hat.

9 Cut a 6-inch (15-cm) piece of ribbon. Glue the two ends of the ribbon to the back of the hat to form a hanger for the elf.

Do you hear a jingle bell?

125

Pocket Treat Ornament

Surprise your cat or dog on Christmas morning by making this special treat ornament to hang on the tree.

What you need:

old shirt with a pocket

brown pom-pom

large wiggle eyes

thin ribbon

blue glue gel

scissors

jingle bell

brown felt

What you do:

1 Cut the pocket out of an old shirt.

2 Cut ears from the felt that resemble the ears of your cat or dog. They might be floppy ears or they might be pointed ears. Glue the ears to each side of the front of the pocket.

3 Glue the wiggle eyes and a pom-pom nose on the front of the pocket.

4 Cut an 8-inch (20-cm) piece of ribbon. String the jingle bell onto the ribbon, then tie the ribbon in a bow. Glue the bell and the bow to the bottom of the pocket.

5 Cut an 8-inch (20-cm) piece of ribbon to make the hanger. If the pocket you used has a button just tie the ribbon around the space between the button and the shirt, then tie the two ends together. If the pocket does not have a button, cut a tiny slit in the front top and back top of the pocket. String the ribbon through both slits, then tie the two ends together to make a hanger.

Fill the pocket with treats for your pet to enjoy on Christmas morning.

Christmas Eve Moon

*Have you ever seen Santa and his reindeer
flying through the sky on Christmas Eve?*

What you need:

masking
tape

metal
lid from
frozen juice can

scissors

picture of
Santa in his sleigh
with his reindeer from
an old Christmas card

gold thread

yellow-
colored
glue

felt or
construction
paper

white
glue

Styrofoam tray to
work on

What you do:

1 Cut out a small picture of Santa in his sleigh pulled by his reindeer.

2 Fill the indented side of the metal juice lid with the yellow glue to make the moon. Carefully set the picture of Santa partially on one edge of the metal lid to look like it is flying past the moon. Let the project dry completely on the Styrofoam tray.

3 Cut a 4-inch (10-cm) piece of gold thread. Put a piece of masking tape on the back of the ornament to create a better gluing surface. Glue the two ends of the thread to the taped back with the white glue to create a hanger for the ornament. Cover the thread ends with another piece of tape to hold them in place while the glue dries. If you wish, you may cover the back of the ornament with a circle of felt or construction paper.

Merry Christmas, Santa!

Little Candle

Candles are a symbol of the light that came into the world with the birth of the baby Jesus.

What you need:

golf tee

masking tape

white glue

Styrofoam tray for drying

straw

yellow or orange pipe cleaner

colored string

sequin shapes

gold glitter

scissors

What you do:

1 Slide the straw over the pointed end of the golf tee. Trim off the extra straw beyond the tip of the tee.

2 Cut a piece of pipe cleaner twice as long as the straw piece. Fold the pipe cleaner in half. Cover the two ends with glue and slide it down into the straw on one side of the golf tee. Leave about a $\frac{1}{2}$-inch (1-cm) piece of the fold sticking out at the top to form the flame.

3 If the straw you used is plastic instead of paper, you will need to wrap it in masking tape to create a better gluing surface.

4 Cover the taped straw with glue, then sprinkle it with gold glitter. Glue one or more shaped sequins on to decorate the candle. Let dry on the Styrofoam tray.

5 When the project is dry, thread a 5-inch (13-cm) piece of string through the fold of the pipe cleaner flame. Tie the two ends of the string together to make a hanger.

Make lots of little candles using different color glitters and sequin shapes.

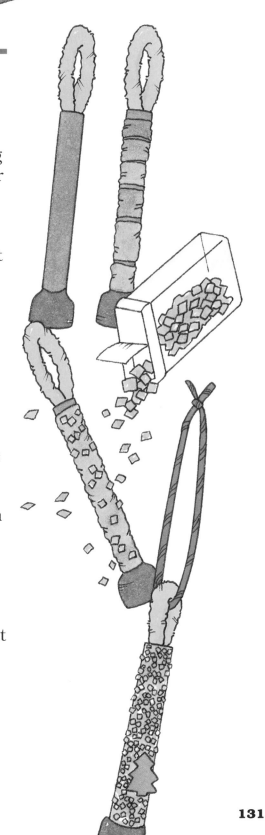

Glue Disk Ornament

Use different color combinations to make an endless variety of these glue disks.

What you need:

white glue

3- to 4-inch (8- to 10-cm) plastic lid

margarine tub and craft stick for mixing

colored string

sequins and glitter

food coloring

scissors

Styrofoam tray to work on

What you do:

1 Pour about ½ cup of glue into the margarine tub. Color the glue with several drops of food coloring. Mix the glue and coloring with the craft stick until the glue is evenly colored.

2 Place the plastic lid on the Styrofoam tray. Pour the colored glue into the lid to fill it without causing the glue to overflow.

3 Cut a 4-inch (10-cm)-long piece of string. Press the two ends of the string into the glue at the edge of the ornament to make a hanger.

4 Decorate the glue with sequins and glitter. Let the glue dry completely. This could take up to a week. Make sure you have put this ornament on a flat surface to dry, or the glue will run over on the lower side. Remove the dried glue ornament from the lid and it is ready to hang on your Christmas tree.

You could use the same idea with tiny plastic lids to make mini ornaments for a tabletop tree.

Snowman in a Sleigh

Anyone for a sleigh ride?

What you need:

three cotton balls

old mitten or glove

red poster paint and a paintbrush

cardboard egg carton

scissors

12-inch (30-cm) red pipe cleaner

white glue

tiny pom-pom

two wiggle eyes

sequins

green yarn

Styrofoam tray to work on

hole punch

What you do:

1 To make the sleigh, cut a single cup from the egg carton, leaving one side higher than the other to form the back of the sleigh. Paint the entire egg cup red. Let it dry on the Styrofoam tray.

2 Cut the pipe cleaner in half. Shape the two pieces along the bottom of the egg cup to make runners curving up the high side and curving down at the ends to form handles on the sleigh. Glue the pipe cleaners in place on the sleigh.

3 Punch a hole in the back, high side of the sleigh, between the handles. Tie a piece of yarn through the hole to make a hanger for the ornament.

4 Glue three cotton balls together to make a snowman.

5 Cut a 1-inch (2½-cm) piece from the tip of the thumb of the mitten or glove. Glue the tip on the head of the snowman for a hat. Glue the pom-pom on top of the hat.

6 Tie a yarn scarf around the neck of the snowman. Glue on two wiggle eyes and some sequin buttons.

7 Glue the snowman in the sleigh, ready to go for a ride.

You might want to decorate the sleigh with sequins, too.

135

Pasta Candy Cane

Candy canes are always
a festive addition to a tree.

🖊 What you need:

small tube-shaped pasta

scissors

red poster paint and a paintbrush

6-inch (15-cm) red pipe cleaner

green yarn

thin red ribbon

Styrofoam tray to work on

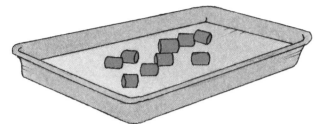

What you do:

1 Paint nine tube pastas red. Let them dry on the Styrofoam tray.

2 String one red pasta to the end of the pipe cleaner. Fold the end of the pipe cleaner over to hold the pasta on the pipe cleaner.

3 Alternate stringing natural-colored pasta with the red pasta, ending with a red one. Fold the end of the pipe cleaner over to hold the pasta on the pipe cleaner. Bend the pipe cleaner into a candy-cane shape.

4 Tie a piece of thin ribbon in a bow around the candy cane.

5 Cut a 5-inch (13-cm) piece of the green yarn. Tie the yarn around the top of the candy cane. Tie the two ends together to make a hanger for the ornament.

This decoration is yummy looking—but don't take a bite!

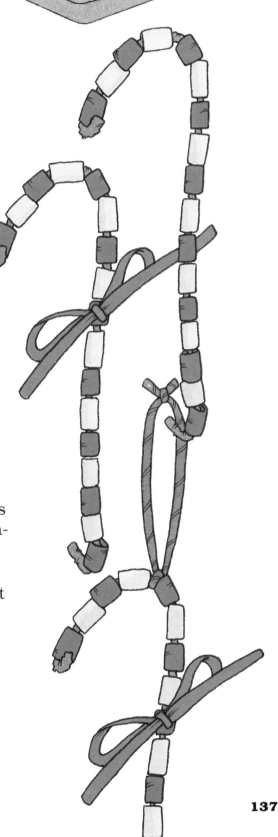

Egg Mouse

Make this little mouse to nestle in the branches of your tree.

What you need:

plastic egg left over from Easter

paper napkin with a design all over it

scissors

small pom-pom

poster paint with paintbrush

two medium flat buttons

two wiggle eyes

water

white glue

clothespin

masking tape

Styrofoam tray for drying

plastic bowl for mixing

black pipe cleaner

newspaper to work on

What you do:

1 Cut a 5-inch (13-cm) piece of pipe cleaner. Tape the pipe cleaner to one side of the egg so that it will stick out the end for a tail for the mouse.

2 Cut a piece out of the napkin large enough to completely cover the egg. Thin $\frac{1}{4}$ cup of glue with a few drops of water in the plastic bowl. Dip the napkin in the watery glue to completely cover it. Wrap the egg in the gluey napkin, smoothing down any excess edges. Make sure you leave the tail sticking out from one end.

3 Put a piece of masking tape on the back of each button to create a better gluing surface. Glue the buttons to the head end of the mouse for ears. Glue on the two wiggle eyes and a pom-pom nose. Let the egg mouse dry on the Styrofoam tray.

4 Paint the clothespin in a color that matches the print on your napkin.

5 Glue the mouse to a flat side of the clothespin.

Use the clothespin to clamp the mouse to a branch of your tree.

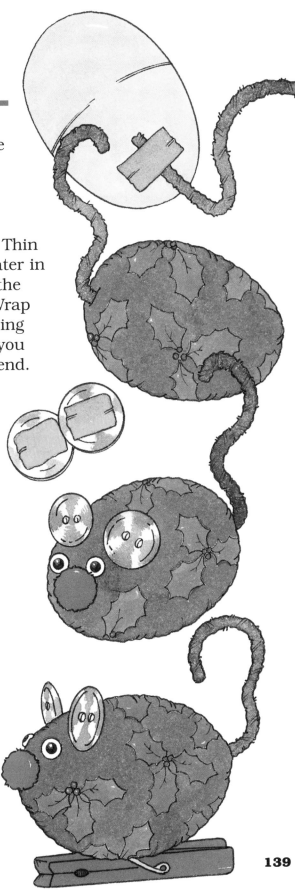

Pipe Cleaner Pine Bough

This tiny bough will not lose its needles like a real one.

What you need:

brown and green pipe cleaners

red thread

thin red ribbon

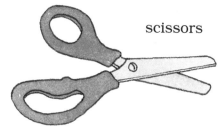

scissors

What you do:

1 Cut a 5-inch (13-cm) piece of brown pipe cleaner. Bend it so that 3 inches (8 cm) hang down on one side and 2 inches (5 cm) on the other.

2 Cut several 1½-inch (4-cm) pieces of green pipe cleaner. Wrap the pieces around the two brown pipe cleaner branches to make the pine needles. Turn the end of each brown pipe cleaner up over the last green needle to keep the needles from slipping off the branches.

3 Tie a piece of red ribbon in a bow around the fold of the brown pipe cleaner.

4 Cut a 5-inch (13-cm) piece of red thread. Tie the thread around the fold of the brown pipe cleaner, then tie the two ends together to make a hanger for the ornament.

You might also want to tie on a tiny pinecone or jingle bell with the red ribbon.

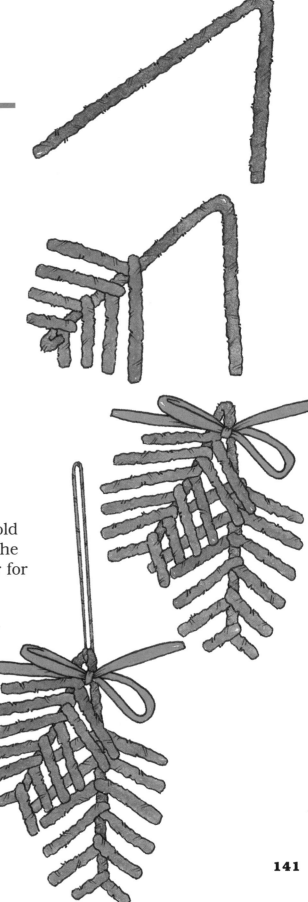

Deck the Halls!

Bow Tree

Last year's package bows can be turned into a charming decoration for this year.

What you need:

twelve pre-made package bows in various sizes and colors

green poster board (or you can paint white poster board green)

white glue

scissors

pencil

white rickrack

green yarn

hole punch

red felt scrap

What you do:

1 Arrange the bows on the poster board in the triangle shape of a Christmas tree. Use the larger bows along the bottom of the tree. Glue the bows in place. Let the glue dry before continuing.

2 Use the pencil to draw the outline of the tree around the bows. Add a trunk to the bottom of the tree. Cut out the tree.

3 Cut a pretty base for the bottom of the tree from the red felt. Glue the base over the trunk of the tree. Decorate the base with rickrack.

4 Cut a 6-inch (15-cm) piece of yarn to make a hanger for the tree. Punch a hole through the top of the tree. Thread one end of the yarn through the hole and tie the two ends together.

If you have a very large supply of bows, you might want to try making a bigger tree.

Button Tree Magnet

*These magnets are so easy to make
that you can quickly make some to keep
and some to give as gifts.*

What you need:

lots of different buttons

green poster board

white glue

scissors

sparkle stem

sticky-back magnet

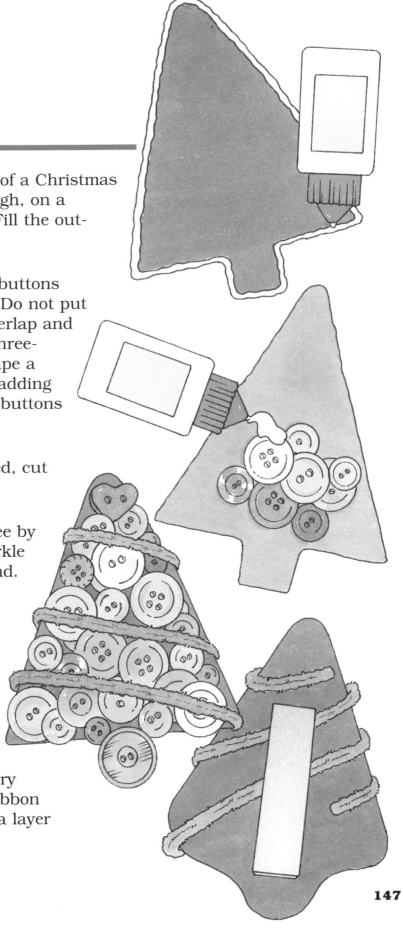

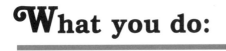What you do:

1 Squeeze a glue outline of a Christmas tree, 3 inches (8 cm) high, on a piece of poster board. Fill the outline in with glue.

2 Sprinkle the glue with buttons to make a button tree. Do not put the buttons on flat. Overlap and stack them for a nice three-dimensional effect. Shape a tree with your fingers, adding more glue over the top buttons if needed.

3 When the glue has dried, cut the tree shape out.

4 Decorate the button tree by wrapping it with a sparkle stem to look like garland.

5 Press a strip of sticky-back magnet on the back of the tree.

Make lots of button trees to decorate your refrigerator. Think of other ways to decorate the trees. Try wrapping one in thin ribbon or sprinkling one with a layer of clear glitter.

Holly Christmas Card Line

Hang all those pretty Christmas cards up for everyone to enjoy.

What you need:

spool of
green ribbon,
1-inch (2.5-cm) wide

Styrofoam trays for
drying

red and green
construction paper

white
glue

148 clothespin for
each card

scissors

What you do:

1 Cut a 4-inch (10-cm) holly leaf from the green paper for each clothespin you are decorating. Glue a leaf to one side of each clothespin.

2 Cut three small berries from the red paper for each holly leaf. Glue the berries to the bottom of the holly leaf, at the clamp end of each clothespin. Let the clothespins dry on the Styrofoam tray.

3 Cut a length of green ribbon slightly longer than you want your card display to be. Tie each end of the ribbon to a secure place such as a curtain rod. Use a holly-covered clothespin to hang up each Christmas card you receive.

This is a decoration that gets prettier and prettier as you add more cards to it each day until Christmas.

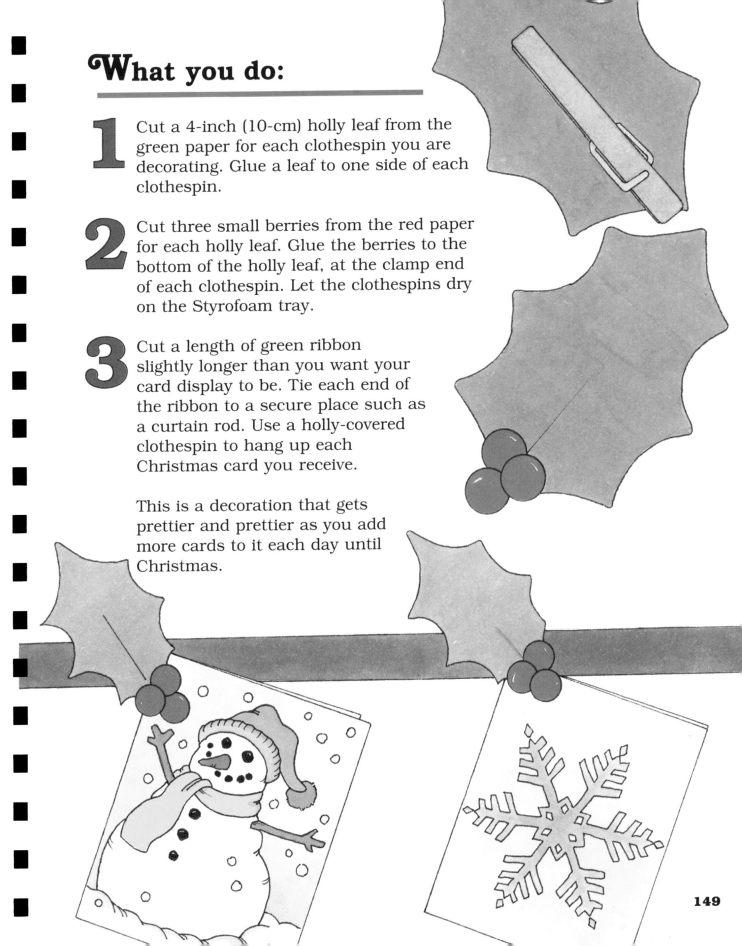

Santa Tissue Box

Turn a tissue box into a cheerful Santa for the holidays.

What you need:

square shaped tissue box with tissue still in it

fiberfill or cotton balls

red, white, black, and pink construction paper

white glue

scissors

What you do:

1 Turn the box on its side and pull the first tissue partway out to form the beard for the Santa.

2 Cut a triangle-shaped hat from the red construction paper and glue it to the edge of the box above the beard.

3 Cut cheeks from the pink paper, eyes from the black and the white paper, and a nose from the red paper. Glue the facial features on the space between the beard and the hat.

4 Use the fiberfill or cotton balls to make hair on each side of the face and fur trim for the bottom edge and top tip of the hat.

Tissue box Santas make delightful and useful gifts for the holiday season.

Soft-Sculpture Snowman

This happy and huggable snowman wants to decorate your room this Christmas season.

What you need:

adult large-size
white T-shirt

big red
pom-pom

colorful old
adult-size sock

fabric scrap

red, green, black,
and orange felt

four sturdy
rubber bands

white
glue

bag of
fiberfill

scissors

What you do:

1 Push the sleeves to the inside of the shirt. Gather the fabric around the neck opening and hold it together with a rubber band. Stuff the top part of the shirt with fiberfill for the head of the snowman. Use a rubber band to hold the head stuffing in place and form the neck.

2 Stuff the bottom of the shirt with fiberfill. Close the bottom of the snowman with a rubber band.

3 Cut the cuff off the colorful sock to make a hat for the snowman. Pull the cuff down over the gathered neck of the shirt at the top of the snowman. Glue the cuff hat in place. Roll the bottom edge of the cuff up to form the brim of the hat. Close the top of the cuff with a rubber band. Glue the red pom-pom at the top of the hat.

4 Use the fabric scrap to cut a scarf for the snowman, and tie it around his neck.

5 Cut a carrot nose for the snowman from the orange felt. Cut circles of black felt for the eyes, mouth, and buttons of the snowman. Glue the face pieces and buttons on the snowman.

6 Give the snowman a Christmasy look by cutting two holly leaves from the green felt and some holly berries from the red felt. Glue the holly on one side of the snowman.

This snowman will not melt, even when you give him a Christmas hug!

Christmas Stocking Pencil Holder

Make this project to decorate your desk for the holidays.

What you need:

toddler-size red sock

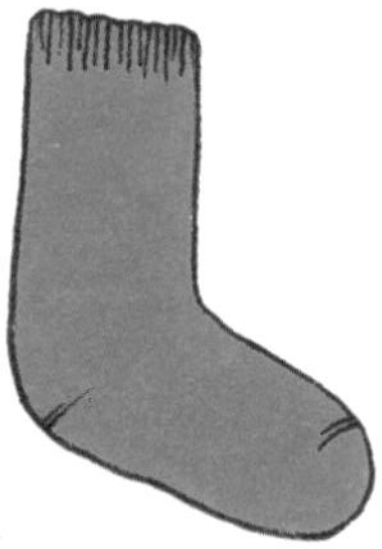

cardboard toilet-tissue tube

fiberfill

two red sequins

white glue

green felt scrap

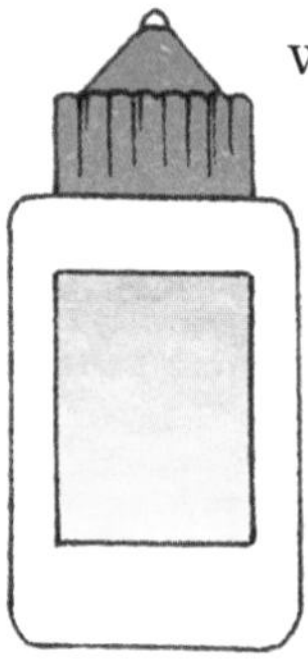

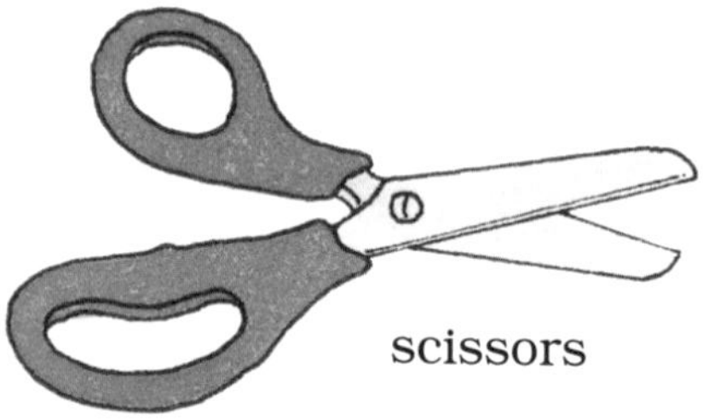

scissors

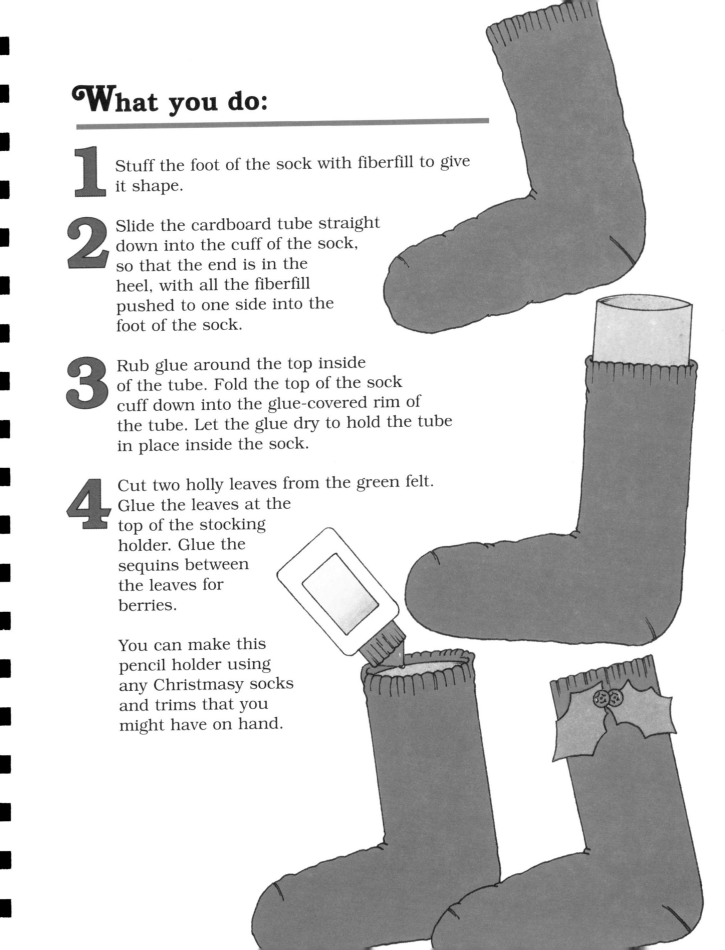

What you do:

1 Stuff the foot of the sock with fiberfill to give it shape.

2 Slide the cardboard tube straight down into the cuff of the sock, so that the end is in the heel, with all the fiberfill pushed to one side into the foot of the sock.

3 Rub glue around the top inside of the tube. Fold the top of the sock cuff down into the glue-covered rim of the tube. Let the glue dry to hold the tube in place inside the sock.

4 Cut two holly leaves from the green felt. Glue the leaves at the top of the stocking holder. Glue the sequins between the leaves for berries.

You can make this pencil holder using any Christmasy socks and trims that you might have on hand.

Shelf Elf

Make this little elf to sit on the edge of your shelf or mantel.

What you need:

cereal box

cellophane tape

jingle bell

pencil

red and white pipe cleaners

red rickrack

two wiggle eyes

white glue

fiberfill

green and pink construction paper

small red and large green pom-poms

scissors

What you do:

1 Starting at one corner of the bottom of the box, cut a triangle shaped corner from the box with the cut side of the triangle being about as long as the bottom of the box.

2 Cover the front, back, and sides of the box with green paper. Do this by tracing around each side of the box with a pencil and cutting out each resulting shape to glue over the side you traced.

3 Cut a round face from the pink construction paper. Glue it to one side of the box about 1½ inches (4 cm) below the point at the top of the triangle.

4 Glue a strip of rickrack across the top of the head to form the bottom of a pointed hat for the elf. Glue the large green pom-pom to the top of the hat.

5 Glue the two wiggle eyes and the red pom-pom nose to the face. Glue fiberfill around the face for hair and a beard.

6 Glue a strip of rickrack across the bottom of the box.

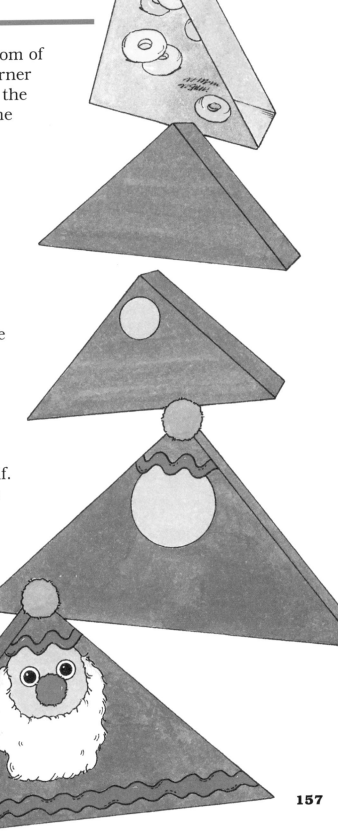

7 Tape the ends of two 12-inch (30-cm) pipe cleaners to the inside front of the box so that they hang down to form legs. Bend the legs forward, then down, to form knees so that the elf can sit with the legs hanging over the edge of a shelf or mantel. Bend the end of each leg forward to make feet.

8 Poke a hole about halfway down each side of the elf. Slip the end of a 6-inch (15-cm) piece of pipe cleaner through each hole to make arms. Tape the ends of the pipe cleaners to the inside of the box elf to hold them in place.

9 Twist 5-inch (13-cm) pieces of red and white pipe cleaner together to make a candy cane for the elf to hold in one hand. Wrap the end of one pipe-cleaner arm around the candy cane to hold it. Slip the jingle bell over the end of the other hand.

Do you hear a bell ringing?

Jingle Bell Napkin Rings

This project looks and sounds like Christmas!

What you need:

6-inch (15-cm) red pipe cleaner for each ring

nine jingle bells for each ring

nine red craft beads for each ring

What you do:

1 String the beads and the jingle bells onto the pipe cleaner, alternating between the two. When they are all on the pipe cleaner, twist the two ends of the pipe cleaner together to form a ring.

You can make your napkin rings all the same or make lots of different ones. Try using different color beads and jingle bells of different sizes. You might even want to buy a package of pretty Christmas napkins and match your pipe cleaner and bead colors to the napkins you chose.

Gift Picture Frame

What better gift than a picture of someone you love?

What you need:

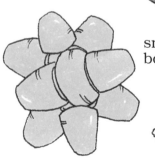

small cardboard box, such as a jewelry box

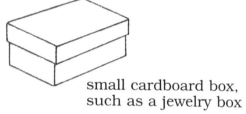

Christmas wrapping paper

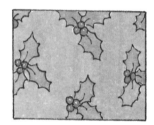

colored tissue paper that looks nice with the wrapping paper

scissors

small package bow

white glue

cellophane tape

photograph

160

What you do:

1 Open the box and wrap the top and the bottom separately, folding the paper down to cover the inside edges of both the bottom and the lid.

2 Glue the bow to the top of the lid.

3 Rub glue all over the inside of the box bottom. Tuck in squares of colored tissue paper in the box so that it covers the bottom and sides of the box and sticks out around the edges like an opened package.

4 Glue a photo in the bottom of the box.

5 Glue the lid of the box at an angle across the top corner of the box bottom. When the glue has dried, stand the box up so that the package becomes a picture frame.

You don't have to wait until Christmas morning to peek inside this package!

Doorknob-Nose Elf

What an unusual nose!

What you need:

two uncoated 9-inch (23-cm) paper plates

garland

red, black, green, and white construction paper

rickrack

poster paint in the skin color of your choice and a paintbrush

paint

pom-pom

red marker

scissors

newspaper to work on

white glue

What you do:

1 Glue the two paper plates together to make a stronger plate.

2 Cut a 4-inch (10-cm) slit across the center of the plate. Cut another 4-inch slit across that slit to form an X-shaped opening that will be used to slip the plate over a doorknob.

3 Paint the bottom side (not the eating side) of the plate for the face of the elf.

4 Cut a piece of garland long enough to go three quarters of the way around the edge of the plate for a beard. Glue the garland beard in place.

5 Cut a triangle-shaped hat for the elf from the green paper. Glue the hat to the top of the elf's head. Decorate the hat with rickrack. Glue the pom-pom to the point of the hat.

6 Cut eyes from the white and black paper. Use the marker to draw a big, happy smile on the elf, then glue a round cheek on each side of the smile.

Give the elf a big shiny nose by slipping the plate over a doorknob.

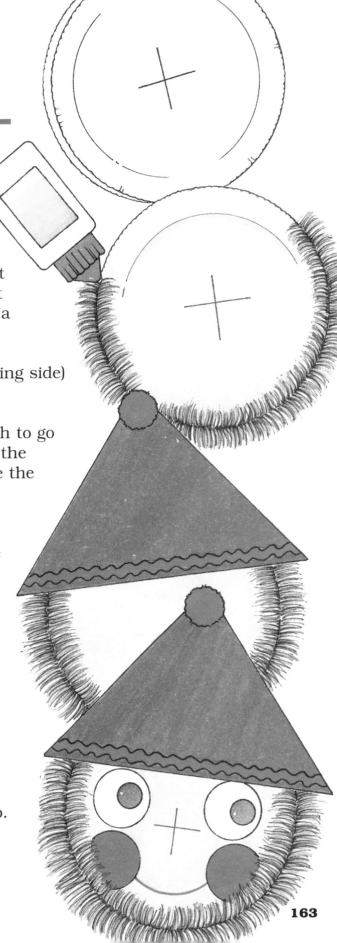

163

Foil Angel

Make this little angel to look just like you!

What you need:

heavy-duty aluminum foil

pencil

white glue

masking tape

pink and yellow construction paper

yarn in your hair color

yarn for a hanger

markers

sparkle stem

scissors

sticker stars

construction paper in skin color of your choice

What you do:

1 Tear off two squares of foil. Fold each square back and forth like a fan to pleat it. Squeeze one folded square of foil together at one end and fan out the other end to make the dress for the angel. Squeeze the other folded square of foil together in the middle and fan out each side for the arms of the dress.

2 Squeeze the neck of the dress and the center of the arms together to attach them. Use masking tape to help secure them together.

3 Cut a 6-inch (15-cm) piece of yarn. Tie the yarn around the neck of the dress, then tie the two ends together to make a hanger for the angel.

4 Cut a construction paper head for the angel. Glue yarn to the head in your hair style. Use the markers to draw a face. Cut heart shaped cheeks from the pink paper and glue them on the face.

5 Shape a halo from the sparkle stem. Use glue and masking tape to attach the stem of the halo to the back of the head.

6 Glue the head over the masking tape at the neck of the dress.

7 Use the pencil to trace your hands on the yellow paper. Cut out both hands. Glue the two hands sticking out from the back of the angel for wings. Place a piece of masking tape over the spot where you will be gluing the wings to create a better gluing surface.

8 Decorate your angel with the sticker stars.

Hang this angel up to remind your favorite grownups how good you've been this year!

165

Stacked Package Christmas Tree

This centerpiece is the perfect project to do as a group to take to a hospital or nursing home during the Christmas season.

What you need:

twenty small empty gelatin or pudding boxes

Christmas wrap in several different patterns

package bow

white glue

cellophane tape

glitter

plastic trash bag to work on

scissors

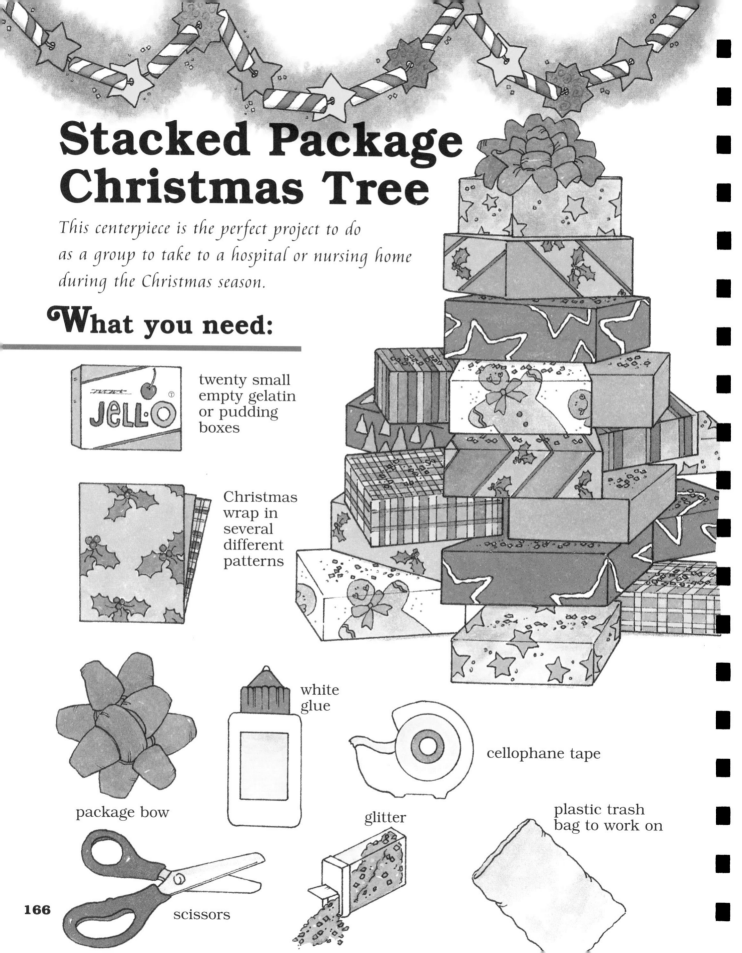

What you do:

1 Close the open end of each box and tape it shut. Wrap each box in Christmas wrap, using a variety of different wraps.

2 Stack the boxes on the plastic bag in a tree shape. Start with four boxes on the bottom, then angle three boxes on top of those, three more layers of three boxes, then two boxes, then two layers of one box. When you are satisfied with the arrangement of the boxes, glue them all together.

3 Dab glue on the exposed areas of the boxes and sprinkle the tree with glitter.

4 Top the package tree by gluing the bow on the top box.

If you are doing this with a group, divide the number of boxes needed by the number of people helping, and ask each person to bring in an assigned number of wrapped boxes. This will give the tree lots of different wrapping paper patterns.

Christmas Memories Box

This project is just what you need to store all those wonderful Christmas memories.

What you need:

Christmas wrapping paper

shoe box with a lid

five large zip-to-close bags

scissors

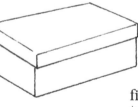

stapler

markers

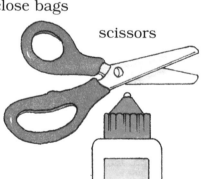

white glue

construction paper in Christmas colors

cellophane tape

What you do:

1 Wrap the lid and the bottom of the box separately in the Christmas wrap.

2 Cut a piece of construction paper to fit inside each of the plastic bags. Line each bag.

3 Cut a piece of paper to fit in the bottom of the box. Staple the paper to the side of one bag, stapling only the back of the bag, behind the liner. Also, staple the paper along the bottom edge of the bag, through both sides of the bag.

4 Staple the side of the next bag to the side of the first bag, making sure that the openings face in the same direction. Staple all the bags together to form a strip of five bags.

5 Cut a piece of paper to fit in the lid of the shoe box. Staple the piece to the side of the last bag in the row, stapling behind the liner. Also, staple the paper along the bottom edge of the bag, through both sides of the bag.

6 Glue the back paper on one end of the row of bags onto the bottom of the box. Glue the back paper on the other end of the row of bags onto the lid of the shoe box. Let the glue dry.

7 Cut Christmas shapes to glue on the lid of the box. Label the box with your name and the year.

Use tape to attach favorite cards, photos, and small favors to the paper liners in the bags. To display your collection, pull the lid out from the box. When Christmas is over, fold your memories back into the box.

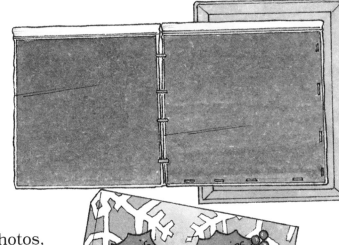

Christmas Carolers

The cluster of carolers makes a charming Christmas decoration.

What you need:

two cardboard paper-towel tubes

two cardboard toilet-tissue tubes

red, green, and white construction paper

Christmas print wrapping paper

cellophane tape

white glue

scissors

rubber band

markers

heavy yarn or fabric scraps

yarn

two colorful child-size socks

two colorful adult-size socks

construction paper in the skin tones of your choice

What you do:

1 Cut one of the two long tubes so that it is an inch or two shorter than the other tube.

2 Cover all four tubes with a different paper, using the wrapping paper and the red and green construction paper. Glue the paper around each tube and hold it in place with cellophane tape.

3 Wrap the top part of each tube with a strip of skin-colored construction paper, gluing it, then securing it with tape.

4 Cut the cuff off each of the four socks to make hats for the carolers. Tie the open end of each cuff closed with a piece of colorful yarn tied in a bow. Glue the cuff hats from the adult socks on the tall tube carolers and the cuff hats from the children's socks on the short tube carolers.

5 Use the markers to draw a face on each caroler.

6 Tie a piece of heavy yarn or a fabric scrap around the neck of each caroler for a scarf.

7 Glue the two tall carolers together side by side. Glue the two short carolers together side by side and in front of the tall carolers. Use a rubber band to hold the carolers together until the glue dries.

8 Cut a music book for each pair of carolers from the white paper. Decorate each book by using the markers. Glue a book in front of each pair of carolers.

"Joy to the world . . ."

171

Wrapping Tube Reindeer

When you finish your holiday wrapping,
you can use the empty tubes to make a reindeer.

What you need:

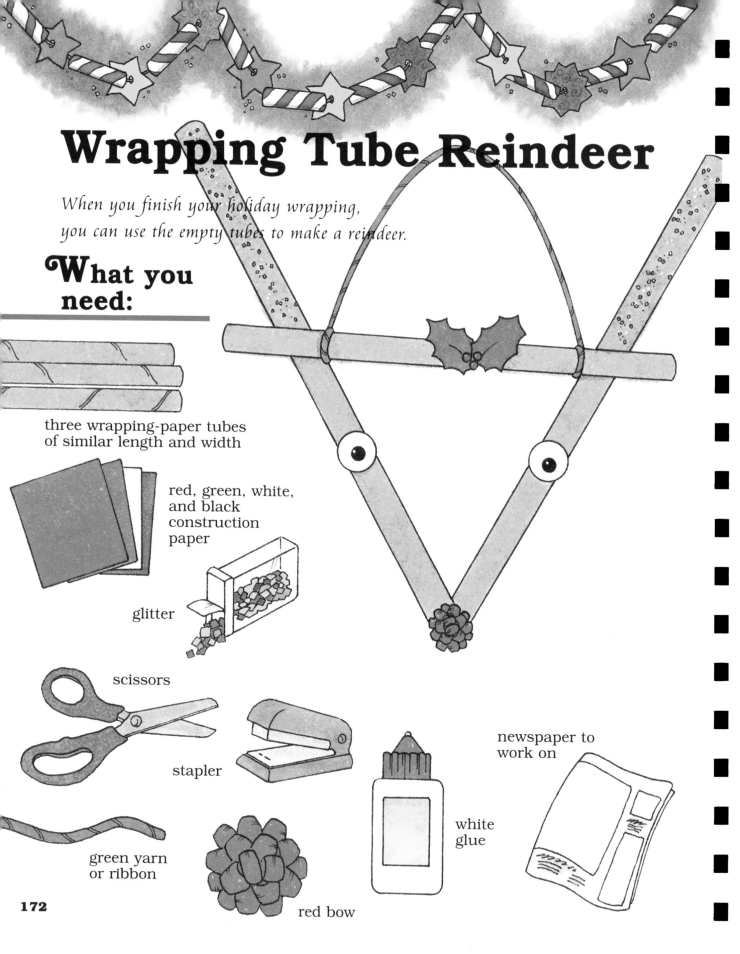

three wrapping-paper tubes
of similar length and width

red, green, white,
and black
construction
paper

glitter

scissors

stapler

green yarn
or ribbon

red bow

white
glue

newspaper to
work on

What you do:

1 Flatten the ends of two tubes and staple them together in a V-shape.

2 Glue the third tube across the middle of the V so that it forms ears and the top half of the V forms antlers.

3 Cut eyes for the reindeer from the black and white paper. Glue an eye to the center of each tube below the ears.

4 Glue the red bow to the point of the V for a red nose.

5 Cut holly leaves from the green paper and berries from the red paper. Glue the holly and berries between the two ears.

6 Rub glue on the antlers and sprinkle them with glitter.

7 Cut a 3-foot (90-cm) length of ribbon or yarn. Tie one end to each ear of the reindeer to make a hanger.

Does the red nose make you think of a very famous reindeer?

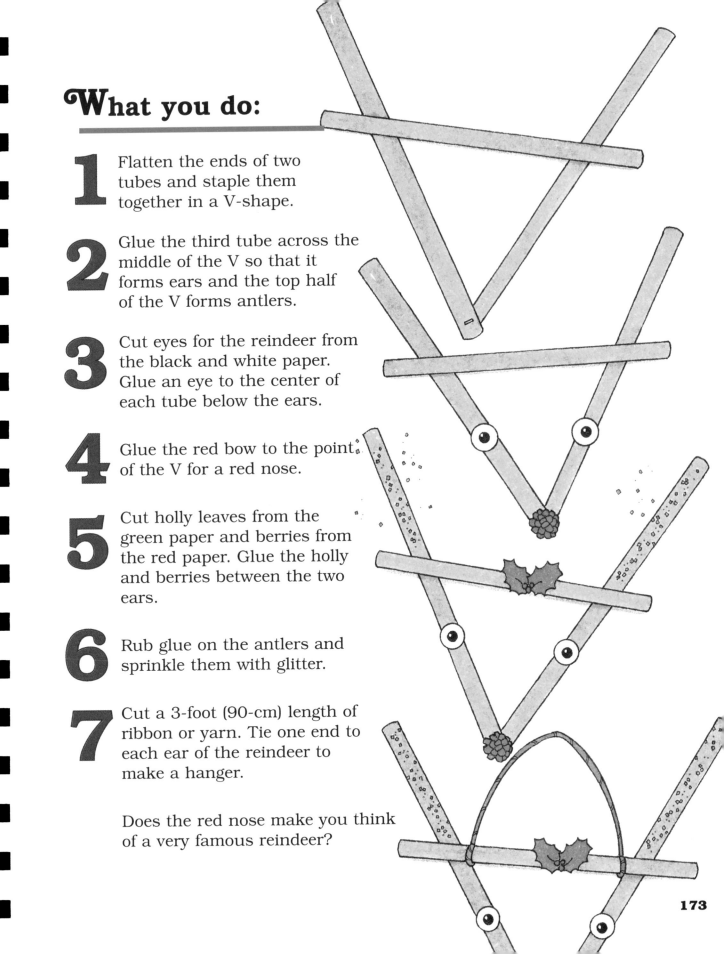

173

Noel Picture Frame

The French word for Christmas is Noël.

What you need:

red and green poster paint and a paintbrush

masking tape

scissors

favorite photo for display

small can from tuna or cat food, emptied and washed

gold garland

white glue

nine craft sticks

pencil

green tissue paper

plastic trash bag to work on

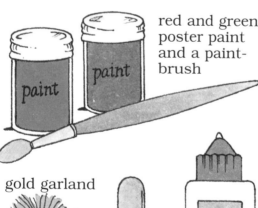

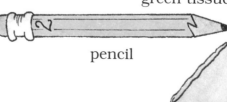

What you do:

1 Glue the sticks together to make an N, E, and L. The tuna can will be the letter O.

2 Paint the stick letters and let them dry on the plastic trash bag.

3 Center the can on the photo. Use the pencil to trace around the can on the photo. Cut out the photo on the traced line.

4 Cover all surfaces of the can, inside and out, with strips of masking tape to create a better gluing surface. Cut a double thickness of green tissue paper large enough to press inside the can to cover it, then wrap down over the sides of the can to cover to the back of the can. Glue the tissue in place to cover the can.

5 Press the photo into the bottom of the can. Use a small dab of glue behind the photo if you need to.

6 Glue two rows of gold garland around the outside of the can.

7 Glue the N to the left side of the can and the E and L on the right side of the can to spell NOEL. Let the project dry face down on the plastic trash bag.

Noel, Noel!

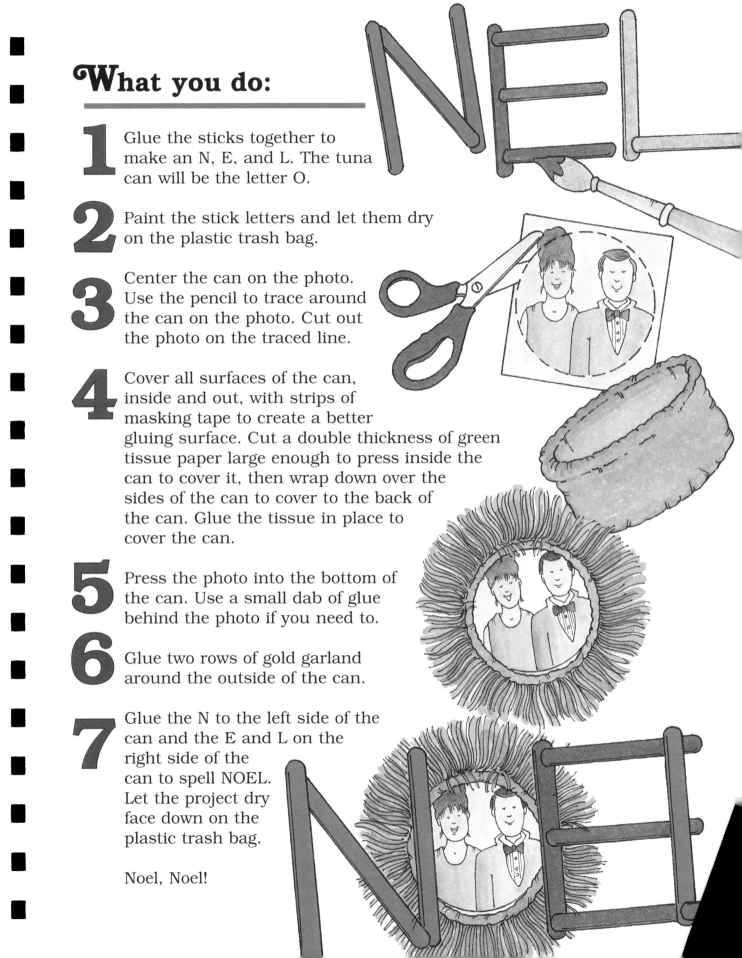

About the Author and Illustrator

Thirty years as a teacher and director of nursery school programs have given Kathy Ross extensive experience in guiding young children through craft projects. Among the more than thirty-five craft books she has written are CRAFTS FOR ALL SEASONS, MAKE YOURSELF A MONSTER, CRAFTS FROM YOUR FAVORITE FAIRY TALES, and CRAFTS FROM YOUR FAVORITE CHILDREN'S SONGS. If you would like to know more about Kathy, visit kathyross.com.

Sharon Lane Holm, a resident of Fairfield, Connecticut, won awards for her work in advertising design before shifting her concentration to children's books. Her recent books include SIDEWALK GAMES AROUND THE WORLD, HAPPY BIRTHDAY, EVERYWHERE!, and HAPPY NEW YEAR, EVERYWHERE! all by Arlene Erlbach, and BEAUTIFUL BATS by Linda Glaser.

Together, Kathy Ross and Sharon Lane Holm have also created the popular *Holiday Crafts for Kids* series as well as the *Crafts for Kids Who Are Wild About* series.